Real Science-4 Kids

Chemistry Connects to
Philosophy

Workbook Level I A

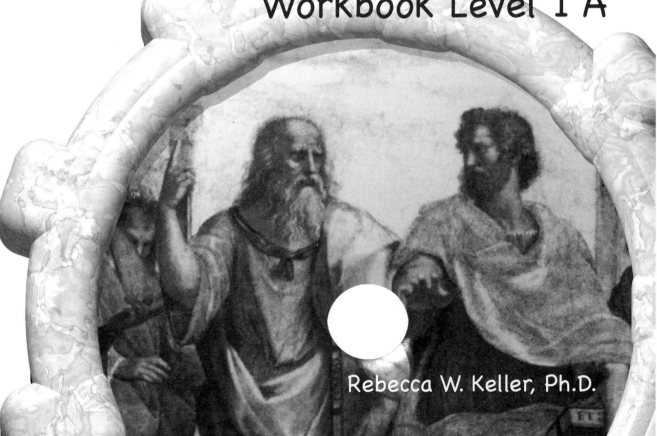

Rebecca W. Keller, Ph.D.

Cover design: David Keller
Opening page: David Keller
Illustrations: Janet Moneymaker, Rebecca Keller
         (unless otherwise noted)
Support Writer: Don Calbreath
Play writer: Dave R. Megill
Editing: Angie Sauberan
Page layout: Kimberly Keller

Real Science-4-Kids/ Kogs-4-Kids™: Chemistry Connects to Philosophy: Level I A

ISBN: 9780979945977

Published by Gravitas Publications, Inc.
P.O. Box 4790
Albuquerque, NM
87196-4790
www.gravitaspublications.com

Printed in the United States of America

Special thanks to G.E. McEwan for valuable input.

Gravitas
Publications Inc.

I Introduction
Philosophy

I.1 What is science?

What is science? Have you ever wondered what science really is or what it is that scientists really do? I am sure you have seen the scientist in the white lab coat who is working furiously with colored test tubes and looking for new discoveries. But is that all there is to science?

Ask yourself, What is science? Then ask your mom or dad and your teacher to give you a definition of science. What did they say? Did you get different answers? If you are having trouble really putting your finger on a definition of science, don't feel bad. The term "science" is hard to define because science involves many different aspects of learning. It involves making observations about nature and designing experiments. It also involves making conclusions and trying to better understand the world we live in.

This is one way to define science:

Science is a systematic way to study the world in which we live.

What does this mean? What is a "systematic way?" Simply put, scientists use systematic, or particular, methods, such as **observation** and **experimentation**, to gain a better understanding of the world around us. Scientists collect information, or **data**, and then they use this data to make conclusions and predictions about how the world works. In today's modern world, scientists also use instrumentation to help them make observations that they can't observe with their senses alone.

There are many ways to define science, but all definitions of science include several systematic steps for the process of scientific inquiry. These include ❶making scientific observations, ❷proposing scientific questions, ❸designing scientific experiments, ❹collecting scientific information, ❺making scientific interpretations, ❻evaluating scientific assumptions, ❼discussing scientific implications, and ❽evaluating different points of view.

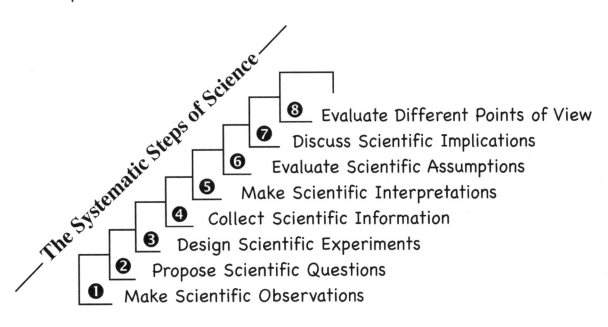

The Systematic Steps of Science

❽ Evaluate Different Points of View
❼ Discuss Scientific Implications
❻ Evaluate Scientific Assumptions
❺ Make Scientific Interpretations
❹ Collect Scientific Information
❸ Design Scientific Experiments
❷ Propose Scientific Questions
❶ Make Scientific Observations

The word "science" is a relatively modern word. That is, you won't find the word "science" in any written documents before about 1400 A.D. The word "science" comes to us from the Latin word *scire,* which means "to know." The word "scientist" was introduced in 1834 by a British scholar named **William Whewell** (1794-1866). Before this time, people who studied science were called "natural philosophers."

Where does science come from? Today's modern science is really a combination of the three different ways that ancient people investigated the world around them. Ancient people first explored the world around them by exploring ideas. Then they explored by observing the things around them. Then they applied their ideas and observations, and they created inventions to help them further explore. Hence, modern science is really a combination of **science as ideas, science as discovery,** and **science as invention.** Science as ideas is now called **philosophy.** Science as discovery is now called a particular scientific discipline, such as **chemistry** or **biology.** And science as invention is now called **technology.**

I.2 What is philosophy?

When we talk about philosophy, we are really referring to the thoughts and ideas that began in the area surrounding the Aegean Sea around 600 B.C. The word "philosophy" comes from the Greek words *philein*, which means "to love," and *soph*, which means "wisdom." So "philosophy" literally means the "love of wisdom."

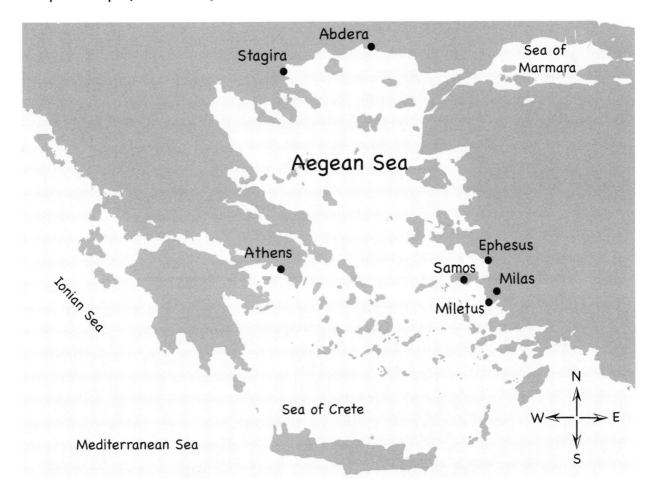

The earliest philosophers were clustered around the Mediterranean Sea, most notably ancient Greece. However, activities that we would today associate with modern science were happening all over the world. Ancient peoples, such as the Egyptians and Native

South Americans, were observing the sky and making mathematical calculations. The Chinese were doing primitive forms of chemistry with mercury and sulfur. And the Native North Americans were testing plants in order to discover which were capable of healing disease and sickness. Today we associate all of these activities, or technologies, with "science."

Before the 15th century, ideas about science (philosophy) and scientific inventions (technology) were largely separate. Philosophers didn't much care for the crafts of inventors, and inventors didn't much care for the lofty ideas of philosophers. These two aspects of modern science did not really overlap in ancient times. Also, chemistry was largely performed by alchemists who didn't overlap with either the philosophers or the inventors.

However, after the 15th century, the philosophical ideas that started in Greece began to merge with the technological discoveries being made by people all over the world. The discoveries made by alchemists began to play a role in both invention and philosophy. For example, with the invention of the telescope, observations about the sky, planets, and stars, that ancient peoples had been gathering for many years, were combined with both math and philosophy that came from Greece and the Middle East. This gave us our current understanding of the planets and solar system. From this time forward, modern science exploded as new discoveries and inventions were put together with philosophical ideas. Science as ideas, science as discovery, and science as invention began to merge together, giving us what we know today as *modern science*.

I.3 Greek philosophers

As we mentioned earlier, scientific thinking got its start in the area around the Aegean Sea with the Greek philosophers. **Thales of Miletus** (*circa* 625-*circa* 545 B.C.) was the first Greek philosopher. After Thales of Miletus, there were **Anaximander** (*circa* 611-*circa* 547 B.C.) and **Anaximenes** (*circa* 585-*circa* 525 B.C.), both from Miletus. Then there were **Heraclitus** of **Ephesus** (*circa* 540-*circa* 475 B.C.), **Pythagoras of Samos** (*circa* 580-*circa*

Thales of Miletus
circa 625-*circa* 545 B.C.

500 B.C.), **Parmenides of Elea** (*circa* 515-*circa* 450), **Empedocles of Acragras** (*circa* 490-*circa* 430 B.C.), **Leucippus of Miletus** (*circa* 480-*circa* 420), and **Democritus of Abdera** (*circa* 460-*circa* 370 B.C.)! What a lot of long names to remember! However, all of these philosophers, in one way or another, had something to offer to science, and we will learn more about them later.

I.4 Socrates, Plato, and Aristotle

However, the three Greek philosophers that had the biggest influence on science and philosophy were **Socrates** (*circa* 470-399 B.C.), **Plato** (*circa* 427-*circa* 347 B.C.), and **Aristotle** (384-322 B.C.). Both Socrates and Plato came from Athens. Aristotle was from Stagira and was the student of Plato. Plato was the student of Socrates. Socrates did not like to study the natural world. He liked to think about human nature instead. Socrates didn't think there was anything valuable to learn by looking at nature.

Socrates
circa 470-399 B.C.

Plato
circa 427-*circa* 347 B.C.

Aristotle
384-322 B.C.

Plato, however, did like to look at nature, and he thought it was important. He began the first school dedicated to both philosophy and natural philosophy. His school was called the Academy. It was located in Athens, and it survived for over 800 years. Plato's most famous student was Aristotle. After Aristotle had studied at the Academy for almost twenty years, he was asked to tutor Alexander, the son of King Philip II of Macedonia. Alexander would go on to become Alexander the Great. Aristotle took the study of natural philosophy even further than his teacher, Plato. Aristotle's work, which included logic, physics, cosmology, anatomy, and even ethics, marked the beginning of a 2000 year history of Aristotelian thought, which dominated much of the Western world.

What is most interesting about these philosophers was not that they got everything right. In fact, many of the ideas they had were simply wrong! However, what they contributed to science was the idea of taking a *rational* and *objective* approach to understanding how the world functions. What we will soon discover is that science progresses through a series of disagreements about how things "are." By using reason, logic, and observation, we can uncover many "facts" about how the world around us works, what it is made of, and how it came into being.

I.5 How science affects philosophy

Philosophers ask the "big" questions. Why is there something, and not nothing at all? Since we are something, where did we come from? What is the meaning of life? What is life? How is life defined? What is the nature of knowledge? How can we know? How do we know that we know? Science, as we have defined it here, is a systematic way of studying the world around us. Scientists collect scientific information, and from that information, they draw conclusions about the world we live in. As scientific information has been collected and understood, some of the questions that philosophers debated in the past, have changed. We no longer debate about the existence of matter. Nor do we debate whether matter is composed of atoms. Scientists have been able to observe and understand some aspects of the nature of matter, like atoms. But other questions, like how did the matter get here in the first place, are still being debated. So science can affect how we think about the world around us.

I.6 How philosophy affects science

But what we think also affects how we do science. If Democritus (a philosopher) hadn't thought that atoms existed, Dalton (a scientist) might not have looked for them. If Aristotle (a philosopher) hadn't thought that the world might be ordered, and that natural laws might exist in an ordered world, Newton (a scientist) might not have looked for such laws. So philosophy, or how we think about the world around us, can affect the science we do. As our thinking changes, scientists will perform different experiments, and they will likely change direction in their search for new discoveries.

I.7 Arguing philosophers

We have seen that philosophy got started in the area around the Aegean Sea around 600 B.C. with Thales of Miletus, but have you ever wondered why? Why did these people develop "philosophy" in the first place? There are several different reasons. One reason that philosophy took off in Greece is that the philosophers liked to argue about everything, especially politics! The Greek philosophers are famous for arguing! They mostly argued about law and justice, but they also argued about government. They used skills, like logic and reason, for their arguments. Eventually, they started arguing about how nature worked. They used the skills of logic and reason for their arguments about nature, and as a result, they started "scientific thinking."

An argument is not just a fight. In fact, the word argue comes from the Latin word *arguere,* which means "to make clear or prove." So an argument is a discussion in which each person tries to prove that he or she is right about something. You might argue with your brother over whose turn it is to have the front seat in your car. If you were a Greek philosopher, you would use logic and reason to prove to your brother that his reasons are flawed, and you would claim the front seat for yourself!

Many people, including scientists and philosophers, are uncomfortable with arguing. They see the world in one way, and they insist that everyone see the world in the same way and often discourage argument and debate. But argument and debate are healthy for science and philosophy. Science, and ways of thinking about and interpreting science, need to be continually challenged, because many new scientific discoveries come from challenging previous scientific conclusions. In this workbook, you will learn about the differing philosophical ideas that shaped our current scientific thinking. You will also learn about the arguments that philosophers and scientists have had over the last several thousand years, as we have been trying to understand the world around us.

I.8 Activity

The Nature of Truth
A Philosophy Play
By D.R. Megill

ARISTOTLE—believed that it is important to study nature to arrive at the truth

SOCRATES—believed that it is more important to study truth to understand nature

PLATO—believed in studying both truth and nature

Socrates and Aristotle are standing on the steps of the Lyceum. They are deep in argument.

ARISTOTLE: I simply mean that, without a close observation of nature, we can't learn anything.

SOCRATES: I understand that is your point, but what is the nature of nature, and what is the nature of what you wish to learn?

ARISTOTLE: Nature is the physical world around us, as well as the mechanics that control it.

SOCRATES: Indeed, I can work with that definition. But as for my second question, since you know so much of this nature, what is it that you wish to learn from observing it?

ARISTOTLE: Well, I wish to learn how it works and why it works. For example, look at this bug, which crosses in front of us. From observing it, we can learn the manner in which bugs move and eat and reproduce and so on.

SOCRATES: Indeed, you are, no doubt, more wise than I in these aspects of nature, but—

ARISTOTLE: I am not fooled by your pretences of humility, Socrates. If you think me a fool, just say so.

SOCRATES: *(softens his tone and speaks sincerely)* I do not think you are a fool, Aristotle. I think many things, but not that. I only meant to say that it appears that you are simply saying that from observing the world around us and the way it works, we can learn about the world around us and the way it works. This is hardly arguable, but tell me, Aristotle, do you think it is more important to know how bugs move or to know what moves people?

ARISTOTLE: Ah, but by observing how bugs move, we may learn of more efficient ways to move people. We can observe differences in movement between the snake, which slithers along on no legs; the fish, which swims; the bird, which flies; and the eight-legged spiders, which crawl. These differences may help us design something yet more ingenious than the wheel itself. Such observations reap profit in technology, Socrates.

SOCRATES: With that segue, let me say that I meant not the locomotion of the body, but what moves the soul and the mind. What does nature tell us about love or justice or piety? Are these things not of inestimably more value, Aristotle? Are these not the true questions of a philosopher?

ARISTOTLE: Indeed, Socrates, you make a good point. But even these things we cannot question directly, for they will not give us an answer. It is only their reactions that we see. So here still, we learn only from the observation of nature.

SOCRATES: Is it not possible, good Aristotle, that we learn these things best not from observation, but from thought, from logic (as you have been so good to name and define for us). It is from rational truths that we will understand what we observe.

(Plato exits the Lyceum and comes upon Socrates and Aristotle. He rolls his eyes when he sees them.)

PLATO: Are you guys still arguing about this? This was the conversation you were having when I went inside. I've had time to teach three math classes and two philosophy classes, engage in some boxing, and meet with the Olympics Committee, and you two are no further along than when I left!

SOCRATES: *(smiles)* Ah, dear Plato, you have always been a most impatient and busy fellow. You know that such discussions must follow their own course and must not be rushed to premature conclusions. What say you, Plato? Is it more important to study nature to arrive at the truth or to study truth to arrive at a better understanding of nature?

PLATO: *(sighs)* I don't know why I do this. Neither of you will cease your endless arguing. If eternal things are truly the most valuable, Socrates, you two are assured of a place of value, for your arguments are endless, and the two of you will probably be having this argument across all time! I honestly don't know the answer to your question, but it seems to me that there are eternal things, a point that neither of you actually dispute. Anyway, it seems to me that these eternal things are very important: love, justice, piety, even the gods themselves (or Himself - if as Socrates suggests, there be only one), and so forth. It seems further that the pursuit of these things is the most important pursuit of the philosopher.

SOCRATES: Indeed, you have been a better pupil than your teacher ought to have produced, Plato.

PLATO: But, it also seems to me that a study of nature does teach us about these things. Why, for example, does a rose look and smell pleasing to us? Does it benefit the rose that we like it? Does it benefit us physically that we enjoy its smell? Or, because it is so unnecessarily pleasant to us, does it perhaps tell us of the goodness of providence? I think it may. Thus such studies may teach us of order, justice, goodness, love, and even God himself. So is it useful to study nature? I say yes.

ARISTOTLE: Indeed, you seem to have overreached your own teacher.

PLATO: But it is not useful to study nature only for its own sake. Rather, it is important to study nature in order to understand the universal ideas and truths that Socrates proclaims, but that you too soon dismiss, Aristotle.

SOCRATES: So, friend Aristotle, you see that I have at least one witness to my position that the study of the universals is what matters most.

ARISTOTLE: It seems to me, Socrates, that surprisingly, for being your student, Plato rather leans toward my way of thinking.

SOCRATES: Hmm, perhaps your skills of observation are not quite waxing in your waning years. Or perhaps it is my poor ears that are growing deafer, but I heard him differently. Be that as it may, enlighten me further. Let me ask you a few questions. What is the nature of the nature that you observe? And when you observe, do you use the nature of your eyes or the curiosity of your soul? And furthermore. . . .

PLATO: *(laughs)* Well, you guys enjoy your argument. I'm going to explore the nature of a fine meal at the Gyros down the way. Plato exits laughing while Aristotle and Socrates continue their argument.

(end)

● I.9 Discussion questions

1. Think about a situation where you needed to argue your side with a sibling or friend. Describe how you feel as you think about arguing your side. Do you feel calm or anxious? Do you feel excited or scared? Describe what happens in your body as you think about arguing your side. What do you think would help you to stay calm as you try to make your argument?

_____

_____

_____

●_____

_____

_____

2. Think about a situation where you needed to argue your side with a parent, teacher, or another adult. Describe how you feel as you think about arguing your side. Do you feel calm or anxious? Do you feel excited or scared? Describe what happens in your body as you think about arguing your side. What do you think would help you to stay calm as you try to make your argument?

_____

_____

●_____

3. Is it easier to argue your side with a friend/sibling or with a parent/other adult? Why?

_____

_____

_____

_____

_____

4. Imagine that you are a young Einstein working as a patent clerk in a patent office. You come up with a radical new idea for how light and matter interact. How would you argue for your discovery, which goes against the standard scientific theories of the day and is opposed by many established scientists?

_____

_____

_____

_____

_____

_____

_____

_____

1 The Elements

Philosophy

1.1 Introduction

Humans have always asked questions about the "stuff" around them. Some of the questions were practical, such as asking what we could use for food or clothing. Other questions were concerned with what we could use to build shelter. Money is always important, so gold and silver were of great interest.

Other questions humans have asked have dealt with more basic issues. What is all this "stuff" made of? In modern times, we are able to go into a laboratory and measure what is in a particular material. However, this ability was not available until the last couple of centuries. The ancient philosophers thought a lot about many issues. In the introduction, we learned that the word "philosopher" comes from two Greek words, and it means "love of wisdom." Philosophers ask difficult questions and try to answer them.

Philosophers think and discuss questions. They don't go into the lab to find answers. For many centuries, there were no labs to do research in. Thinking about questions was the only approach available.

1.2 Famous philosophers

Thales of Miletus (*circa* 625-*circa* 545 B.C.)

The first person that we know about that asked questions about matter was Thales, a Greek philosopher. He did a lot of work in astronomy and mathematics. He was born in a small trading town on the Aegean Coast called Miletus. Thales is believed to have traveled to Egypt, where he learned geometry and astronomy from the Egyptians. He is credited with bringing this knowledge back to Greece. He used what he knew about the stars to his advantage. One story has it that he bought olive presses because he predicted a large olive harvest. He was right! He made lots of money selling olive oil to everyone!

Thales believed that water was the fundamental unit of matter. He thought that everything in the universe came from water. Thales also felt that water could turn into earth and other types of matter.

Thales was one of the first people to describe astronomy and other sciences as natural behaviors. He did not believe that the gods had any influence on the earth, the weather, the tides, or the stars.

Anaximander (*circa* 611-*circa* 547 B.C.)
Many of the philosophers, which lived during the time that Anaximander was alive, were looking for the essence (the true nature of a thing) of all things. What is everything composed of? Anaximander came up with the idea of "the boundless," or "the ultimate." Unfortunately, he never explained what that was. This was not a lot of help to people. Anaximander also studied astronomy. He believed that the earth was

Anaximander
circa 611-*circa* 547 B.C.

hung out in space. He also tried to explain why the earth did not fall. The idea had to do with balance among all the celestial bodies.

Anaximenes
circa 585-*circa* 525 B.C.

Anaximenes (*circa* 585-*circa* 525 B.C.)
In contrast to Thales, Anaximenes believed that air was the basic substance of matter. According to Anaximenes, when air was thinned, it could become fire. In addition, if air was condensed, it would become wind and clouds. And more condensing would compress air into water, earth, and even stone. Many natural processes were "explained" by Anaximenes's theory that air was the basic substance of matter. For example, he believed that thunder and lightning came from wind breaking out of clouds, that rainbows occurred when the sun's rays hit the clouds, and that earthquakes took place when the ground dried out after a rainstorm.

Empedocles (*circa* 490-*circa* 430 B.C.)

Empedocles was all things to all people. Some people believed he was a great healer. Others thought he was a magician. He had some convinced he was a living god. And others believed he was a total fake. The "periodic table" of earth, air, fire, and water came from Empedocles. He believed that these four "roots" made up all matter. He believed that even living creatures were composed of these materials.

Empedocles
circa 490-*circa* 430 B.C.

Leucippus (*circa* 480-*circa* 420 B.C.)

We don't know much about Leucippus. He apparently was the first person to suggest the idea of empty space. (Today, we would call this a "vacuum.") He also developed the idea of atoms. Leucippus believed that the different atoms had different sizes and weights. We now know this to be true.

Democritus (*circa* 460-*circa* 370 B.C.)

Probably one of the first weather forecasters, Democritus had people convinced that he could predict the future. He was a student of Leucippus, and he is an example of a pupil that is better known than his teacher. He studied a lot of natural objects, and he gave public lectures.

The Greek philosophers debated about a lot of things. One of their debates had to do with sand on the beach. They asked the following questions: Can you divide a grain of sand indefinitely? and Is there a point where you have to stop breaking the grain in half?

Most of the philosophers believed that you could divide the grain of sand continuously, without ever stopping. Democritus, however, believed that there was a point at which the grain of sand could no longer be broken into smaller pieces. He called this smallest piece of matter the **atom**, meaning "indivisible."

Many philosophers thought about moral ideas along with their science. Democritus also did this. He believed that happiness came from an even temperament. From this idea, he came up with his list of what was right and what was wrong.

1.3 What are things made of?

The early Greek philosophers had many arguments over many centuries. They argued about how the world works, how it was made, and how it came into being. Modern natural philosophers, or scientists, still use reason, logic, and observation to argue about many of the same questions that the Greek philosophers argued about some 2500 years ago.

One of the topics that these early Greek philosophers disagreed about was what the world was made of. They each had their own ideas.

As we saw earlier, Thales thought that everything was made of water. He believed that water was the "primary substance" of all things. He thought that water could not be divided any further. Today we know that water is made of two hydrogen atoms and one oxygen atom.

Anaximander rejected water as the primary substance. As we saw earlier, he thought that everything was made of something that he called "the boundless." Nobody is really sure what Anaximander meant by "the boundless," and this caused problems for him.

Anaximenes didn't agree with either Thales or Anaximander. He rejected both water and "the boundless" as the primary substance. He believed that air was the primary substance.

Empedocles disagreed with everyone, and he said that all of the things in the world were made up of not just one substance, but of four: earth, air, fire, and water.

1.4 Democritus and Leucippus

There were two other philosophers, Democritus and Leucippus, who didn't agree with any of the other philosophers. Democritus and Leucippus thought that the world was made up of "atoms." They had trouble explaining exactly what atoms were because they didn't know anything about them. However, they thought that all things were made of one type of thing, which they called an atom. They thought that atoms could be combined, like legos, to make larger things.

Today we know that Democritus and Leucippus were right and that the other philosophers were wrong. But Democritus and Leucippus didn't get very many people to agree with them. Atoms were not considered a serious possibility until the 17th century, almost 2000 years later! Let's meet some of these philosophers in a *hypothetical* argument. Hypothetical means that it didn't really happen this way- it's just pretend and just for fun!

1.5 Activity

The Mystery of Substance
A Philosophy Play
By D. R. Megill

ANAXIMANDER—believed everything is made up of "the boundless"

ANAXIMENES—believed everything is made up of air

THALES—believed everything is made up of water

DEMOCRITUS—believed everything is made up of atoms

Anaximander, Anaximenes, and Thales are having a heated argument. They are standing in a circle in the center of the city. Democritus is sitting on the ground building, or playing, with some sort of weird, unrecognizable materials [legos]. It appears that Democritus is barely listening.

THALES: But it's obvious that everything comes from water! The very nature of life speaks to this. We could not live without water! Notice what happens when water is absent from a land for any period of time! It becomes barren, empty. Everything dies. Other forms of life come from water too: fish, frogs, and so on. Even our friend Democritus here on the ground (What are you doing, Dem?) must come from water.

ANAXIMANDER: But surely you see that there are things that could not possibly come from water. Things like earth and fire most certainly do not come from water.

THALES: Hmmm. Yes, fire presents a difficulty, considering that water destroys fire.

ANAXIMENES: I think you may have water on the brain, Thales. Rain drops from air. Thus, I am convinced by this, and by other proofs, that air is the source of all things! Air may take on different forms according to its different properties. In a rarefied form, it could even become fire. Fire can be destroyed not only by the addition of water, but more importantly, by the subtraction of air. This again, is proof of my point!

ANAXIMANDER: If Thales's head is full of water, does that mean yours is full of air, friend Anaximenes? I fear you are both wrong, but I don't fault you for it. It is very difficult to identify what things are made of.

THALES: You feel, no doubt, that you have done so?

ANAXIMANDER: Truth be told, yes, I have. It is hard to identify because we do not see it. We see only the parts into which it has been broken. Obviously, if it is the substance from which all things come, we cannot expect to see it in its initial form. We can, though, guess its nature from that which we do see. Tell me, what is true of everything?

ANAXIMENES: Everything has a purpose, I suppose.

THALES: (*looking down at Democritus on the ground*) Democritus here proves otherwise, Anaximenes. He serves no purpose at all, except to tinker with his strange objects.

ANAXIMANDER: No, no, I will tell you what is true of all things. Everything has an opposite! Everything is equally balanced and measured by its opposite. If we could put all these things of opposite nature together, we would get a picture of a perfectly balanced, limitless substance. I call it, therefore, the boundless.

THALES: But what is the boundless, Nax?

ANAXIMANDER: I just told you. It is the thing from which all other things come.

ANAXIMENES: No, you just described it. What is it?

DEMOCRITUS: (*laughing in derision and without looking up*) You will never get the answer to that, my friends. He does not know! He is trying to befuddle you with fancy talk and imprecise terms. He speaks of a boundless, but it is only his imagination that is boundless, not his reasoning. You ask what all things are made of, and he answers that it is that from which all others come. Round and round it goes; where it stops, nobody knows.

ANAXIMANDER: I suppose you could do better then!

DEMOCRITUS: If you truly care to listen to the truth, you would be one of very few.

THALES: Well, I say we let him try, but for Zeus's sake, please stand up and look at us when you talk, as civil people do.

DEMOCRITUS: Well, I never claimed to be civil, but perhaps the argument will be a good break from my current exploration. (*standing up*) You are familiar, I hope, with the only reasonable man in Miletus, Leucippus.

ANAXIMANDER: Of course.

DEMOCRITUS: Well then, if you are familiar with Leucippus, perhaps this will sound familiar to you. I have only followed Leucippus's reasoning and observations to their obvious conclusion. There are two distinct problems. One is the problem of change, and the other is the problem of divisibility.

ANAXIMENES: What?

DEMOCRITUS: Things change. Haven't you noticed? How does a thing change from a basic substance into another thing? How can such a change be possible? As Empedocles of Elea has argued, change is rationally impossible, as it requires the existence of what is not.

ANAXIMANDER: And you accuse me of being obscure!

DEMOCRITUS: Let's leave the problem of change for now, and let's examine the other problem: divisibility. Imagine any element that you regard as the basic substance of things. It matters not what it is. Just imagine it. Now, divide it in half.

THALES: What? But what does that . . .

DEMOCRITUS: Can you do it? Can you picture dividing that substance in half?

THALES: Well, yes, of course, but . . .

DEMOCRITUS: Then that cannot be the basic substance. If it can be divided at all, it is not yet the basic substance. Rather, the two halves that you divided it into are the basic substances. Right?

THALES: Well, yes, you're right. But then, of course, that could be divided again.

DEMOCRITUS: Exactly! I am saying that, by definition, the most basic substance must be that which is no longer divisible.

ANAXIMENES: But no one has ever seen such a thing.

DEMOCRITUS: Of course no one has ever seen such a thing. Such a thing would be invisible to the naked eye. However, when combined with others of its kind, they would become visible. As you can see, the combinations by which these "indivisibles," or atoms, could combine would be virtually numberless, and by combining in different ways, they would make different things. This would explain the appearance of change by things that ultimately do not change.

THALES: Your ideas are nonsense, Democritus.

Democritus begins laughing.

ANAXIMANDER: You are entertaining, Democritus, but obviously, going mad. It's clear by the way you go about laughing at everything all the time.

DEMOCRITUS: If you could see how ridiculous you all are, you and all the others, you would laugh too.

ANAXIMENES: I fear my friends are right. You are clearly either crazy or stupid. These toys of yours, Democritus, what are they?

DEMOCRITUS: I knew you would not listen. Now, if you don't mind, I'd like to get back to my current exploration. *(Democritus kneels back down on the ground.)* If you must know, my nephew invented these. They are a good example of my atomic ideas. These little pieces can be rearranged into various shapes and can be used over and over without any seeming decay. My nephew has named them after his father, my brother, Legosus.

THALES: You have to admit, guys, that water is almost as indivisible as Democritus. I told you I was right.

Anaximander, Anaximenes, and Thales begin walking away from Democritus.

ANAXIMENES: *(to Thales)* You are as crazy as he is.

ANAXIMANDER: I'm telling you, it's the boundless. Let me show you.

(end)

1.6 Discussion questions

1. According to Democritus, what is the primary substance? Explain his description.

_____

_____

_____

_____

_____

_____

_____

_____

_____

_____

2. Do the other philosophers believe Democritus? Why or why not?

_____

_____

_____

_____

_____

_____

_____

_____

3. Imagine that you are on a new planet. Everything on this planet is
   made of candy. What proofs would you use to argue to your friends
   that the basic substance of this planet is candy?

_____

_____

_____

_____

_____

_____

_____

_____

2 How Models Help Us Think
Philosophy

2.1 What is a model?

Most people have a hobby of some sort. Some people like to collect things like stamps or coins or thimbles. Other people like outdoor activities like hiking or skiing or camping. And some people like to build models.

The models could be of anything. Maybe you like model airplanes. Somebody else likes to build model ships. A lot of people like to build model cars.

When we build models, we know they are not the real thing. We understand that they give us an idea of what the real thing looks like, and that idea helps us to understand more about the real thing.

A model in science is the same. We have an idea of what something is, and we use models to help us explain to other people what we are talking about. The model is usually very incomplete. It does not have all of the details of the real thing that we are wanting to understand,

and many times, we don't know exactly what the real thing looks like! So it can be hard to build a model.

One way that scientists use models is to design experiments. Running experiments is important in science, and models help us to decide what experiments we should do. We can test the model by doing experiments that will show us if the model is right or wrong.

2.2 Models and philosophers

For many centuries, people studied the natural world by simply thinking about it. The philosophers spent a great deal of time thinking about what the world was made of. Then they would think of what should happen if their ideas were correct.

The Roman philosopher-poet **Lucretius** (*circa* 99-*circa* 55 B.C.) thought a lot about the atom. He wrote about "primal bodies" that made up everything and that could not be destroyed. Lucretius talked about the different ways the "fastenings of the primordial parts" were put together (chemical bonds?).

"Hook and Eye" Model for Water

René Descartes (1596-1650)

Another philosopher that talked about chemical bonds lived many centuries later. **René Descartes** (1596-1650) talked about hooks and eyes. According to Descartes, some atoms had hooks, and others had eyes. He believed that these two types of atoms could connect with one another.

Descartes talked about hooks and eyes, and people understood what he meant. At the time that Descartes lived, many items of clothing were fastened with hooks and eyes (we didn't have Velcro yet). So the people of his time could hear his theory, and they could have a picture in their minds of what Descartes meant.

The problem was that we could not test Descartes's idea. Descartes had no idea which atoms had hooks and which had eyes. We had no way of actually seeing the atoms to tell if Descartes was right.

2.3 Electrons and chemical bonds

Once electrons were discovered, we had a new way of thinking about chemical bonds. Thinking about these bonds became the domain of the scientist. We could get ideas and go into the lab to test the ideas. Even before electrons were discovered, people were thinking about how atoms were bonding together.

Without even knowing about electrons, **Edward Frankland** (1825-1899) came up with an idea about how atoms might bond! Frankland believed that when atoms bonded in a molecule, both the type of atoms present and the position of the atoms were important.

Some ideas came in strange ways. While he was dreaming, **Friedrich August Kekulé von Stradonitz** (1829-1896) came up with a theory about the structure of a compound called **benzene**. He dreamt about a snake eating its own tail. From this dream, he developed experiments to prove his theory.

Once we learned about electrons and where they were in the atom, we were better able to think about how chemical bonds worked. Our thinking could now be guided by experiments. As we obtained new data, we could develop better chemical bond models.

By thinking about electrons and where they were, scientists could begin to explain the shape of molecules. The location of specific electrons helped to push some atoms away from others. These strains in the molecule helped to determine bond angles and locations of atoms.

2.4 The role of mathematics in chemical bonds

As our ideas about chemical bonds became more complex, we started to use more math to describe where the electrons were in the bond. The math helped us to make predictions that could be tested in the laboratory. But there were problems with these new techniques. The math kept getting more complicated as we tried to fit theory and data together. As a result, our picture of the chemical bond became more specific and more fuzzy at the same time.

A chlorine molecule (Cl_2) model showing a stick bond

Each new idea in the science of chemical bonding made it harder to tell exactly where the electrons in the bond were located. The early model of chemical bonding, which depicted electrons as a stick holding two atoms together, didn't work anymore. We had to develop new models to explain how bonds worked.

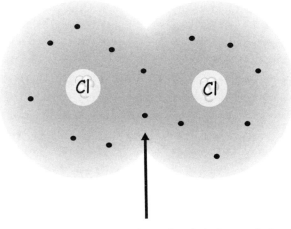

A chlorine molecule (Cl_2) model showing a "fuzzy" bond of two shared electrons in the middle of an orbital

Each new model made the bond look fuzzier. The math gave a picture of **probabilities** for the electron. In other words, how likely (how probable) was it that a specific electron was in a specific area around the atom?

Today, we are back to a lot of philosophical thinking about the chemical bond. We know a lot more than we did one hundred years ago, but at the same time, our new information makes it less certain as to exactly what is happening with the electrons in a chemical bond.

2.5 Computers and chemical models

One very valuable application for computers is in the study of the structure of complex molecules. We can put data about the structure of a molecule into a computer, and it can make a picture of that molecule. The picture can be three-dimensional, and it can give us a very good idea of the structure of that compound.

This technique is extremely helpful in studying how to treat different diseases. We can study how an enzyme works. (Enzymes are proteins that make chemical reactions happen in the body.) If we want to make an enzyme work differently, we can use a computer to help us. We can use computer data to show the enzyme's structure, and the computer data can give us ideas about how to change the way the enzyme functions.

2.6 Activity

Models and Connections
A Philosophy Play
By D.R. Megill

LUCRETIUS—philosopher poet who postulated the existence of only atoms and void

DESCARTES—philosopher who postulated that hooks and barbs hold atoms together

      Famously said, *Cogito Ergo Sum* (I think, therefore I am.)

FRANKLAND—scientist who proposed a new model (called valence) for atomic connections

KEKULÉ—scientist who saw a model for the structure of benzene in a dream

Lucretius, Descartes, Frankland, and Kekulé are all standing in white space. Nothing seems to exist, except them. They all look slightly confused.

LUCRETIUS: Where am I now? What's happened here? It can't be the void. That much is clear. No life after death, at least that's what I've taught. So I don't think I'm dead or I'd have no thought. Before I arrived, on what was I dwelling? Perhaps in that thought is something most telling. Bonds and dreams, these are our themes. What holds things together? And what are the seams?

DESCARTES: Where am I? Who are you? Is this real, or is it a dream? And why are you talking in rhyme?

LUCRETIUS: It can't be the void, because we are here. I am Lucretius, and you're not I fear. Whether real or dream is up to discussion, and I've found rhyming is good for instruction.

FRANKLAND: Lucretius! As in the philosopher poet? Well, I know who I am, and I know who you are. I'm Edward Frankland, and you are altitude sickness. I was on top of Mount Blanc doing experiments with candles, and suddenly I'm here.

DESCARTES: I, also, have heard of Lucretius. But I know that I am not sickness of any kind. On the other hand, you may be the elements of my dreaming. But as for me, I am Descartes, and I know that I am, for I am aware of my own thoughts. I think, therefore I am.

KEKULÉ: Hmmm. How interesting. I was just dozing by my fire. But this dream, or whatever it is, doesn't seem completely random. We are all connected.

DESCARTES: Connected? How?

LUCRETIUS: Bonds and dreams, these are our themes.

KEKULÉ: Indeed, this would not be the first time I've learned from a dream. Once I dreamed I saw a snake biting its own tail, and that dream gave me an understanding of how the atoms in benzene connect together. Likewise, each of us has wrestled with the model for atoms. Each of us has tried to understand how they fit together.

DESCARTES: Hmm, well, let's see if we can put some order to this chaos. Even though this is a dream, it still deserves to be uncluttered, so we can understand it. Lucretius, you believe that everything is comprised of atoms and void, right?

LUCRETIUS: Natural explanations of atoms and void left my theist friends greatly annoyed.

DESCARTES: Indeed. You don't recognize that the existence of external realities necessitates the existence of God. I believe it was your disciple, Democritus, who first posited that hooks and barbs hold atoms together. I worked a bit on that model myself, but most notably, I don't believe in the void you suggest. So, friend Frankland, what's your role in these speculations?

FRANKLAND: Ah, well, I posited the theory of valence. According to my theory, atoms can connect only in certain fashions, and the position of these atoms in a molecule is important. And if I'm not mistaken, this *(indicating Kekulé)* is a contemporary of mine, Kekulé.

DESCARTES: Contemporary. So just what era is contemporary for you?

KEKULÉ: Well, friend Descartes, we are about 300 years after you.

DESCARTES: Well, that can't be. Perhaps you have confused me with someone earlier, like the poet Horace.

KEKULÉ: Oh, no, I'm smarter than that. I know never to put Descartes before the Horace.

FRANKLAND: Oh, that was bad! He's right, René. We are all from various points in history, and yet we remain connected by our search for a model to explain atoms and molecules, the building blocks of everything around us. Perhaps some connections are not bound by time or space? What say you, Descartes?

DESCARTES: I think not! *(Descartes disappears in a puff of smoke.)*

KEKULÉ: Oh ho! Our friend Descartes thought not, and so he was not. I feel it is time for me to wake myself and get back to work. *(Kekulé fades until he disappears.)*

FRANKLAND: Indeed, I really should get back to my experiments on Mont Blanc. *(Frankland disappears.)*

LUCRETIUS:

Bonds and models, connections and dreams,

All is rarely just what it seems.

By models and pictures, we try to draw,

An idea of constructs, substance, and law.

So much we do not understand of what we see,

Like what is the glue that combines A to B,

Or what is the connection betwixt man and man,

Poetry, plays, and models can all lend a hand.

(end)

● 2.7 Discussion questions

1. What advantages do models have for explaining how things work?

_____

_____

_____

_____

_____

_____

_____

●_____

_____

2. What limitations do models have for explaining how things work?

_____

_____

_____

_____

_____

_____

●_____

3. Using the idea of models, describe and/or build a model of the new candy planet that you have recently discovered.

_____

_____

_____

_____

_____

_____

_____

_____

_____

_____

_____

_____

_____

_____

_____

_____

_____

_____

_____

3 Permanence and Predictability
Philosophy

3.1 The world of matter and reactions

When we look at the world around us, we see a lot of things. We see animals, plants, and people. We see cars, houses, video games, clothes, and other material items. All of these things are made up of matter. Because everything is made of matter, and because matter is constantly rearranging, everything has chemical reactions involved with it in some way. Have you ever wondered whether we'll run out of stuff someday?

 Will there always be atoms and molecules, or will they get "used up"? Can we make new atoms and molecules out of nothing, or do we just use the materials we have around us?

3.2 Ancient philosophers and matter

Many ancient thinkers believed that the world was formed from a **"First Matter."** They thought that this material then separated into four elements: earth, air, fire, and water. And they believed that the four elements then remixed in different amounts to make all of the physical matter we see.

The Greek philosopher **Democritus** (*circa* 460–*circa* 370 B.C.) would have been a good chemist. He asked many questions about atoms and matter. Democritus did not know about molecules, but he had some good ideas about matter. The earliest idea about atoms came from Democritus. He believed that atoms existed, and that they could not be divided. He thought that there was no smaller piece of matter than the atom.

Democritus
circa 460–*circa* 370 B.C.

Democritus also thought about matter that was bigger than the atom. He believed that each type of matter had the color or the taste that it did because of the atoms in it. He believed that the specific atoms that made the matter (like the atoms that make butter) would interact with the atoms in our bodies (and we would taste butter). The idea of matter changing was an idea that not all philosophers agreed upon. **Heraclitus** (*circa* 540–*circa* 475 B.C.) believed that everything changes, and so he believed that matter could change. **Parmenides** (*circa* 515–*circa* 450 B.C.), on the other hand, believed that nothing changes, and so he believed that matter would never change. So who was right?

3.3 Alchemists and chemical reactions

The **alchemists** believed a lot of the ideas of the ancient philosophers. They agreed with Heraclitus's position that everything changes, and they thought that lead could be returned to the "First Matter." They believed that once it was returned to the "First Matter," it could then be rearranged to make gold.

But the alchemists did not understand about chemical reactions. They thought that they could change one type of atom into another. They didn't know that, in some ways, both Heraclitus and Parmenides were right. Some things can change, but not everything can change, and the alchemists could not change lead atoms into gold atoms.

3.4 Chemical reactions and atomic theory

By the time **John Dalton** (1766-1844) came up with his atomic theory, there were already some facts known about chemical reactions. People knew that materials could be changed into other materials, but it looked like certain substances were lost in those changes.

For example, when wood was burned, ashes were left. But the ashes weighed a lot less than the wood. It looked like there was a lot of matter lost in the reaction. But what wasn't known was that matter wasn't lost; it was just not all accounted for because not all of the chemicals involved in chemical reactions were known.

Dalton and others realized that the burning wood gave off gases. We can't see these gases, but we can show that they exist. When wood burns, part of the chemical reaction involves making an invisible substance, and that substance has some of the atoms that were in the original wood. Part of Dalton's atomic

theory involved the idea of molecules. Dalton said that atoms were
not created or destroyed in a chemical reaction; the atoms were just
rearranged into different combinations. So the atoms don't change; only their
arrangement changes. So again, Heraclitus and Parmenides were both right!

Antoine Lavoisier (1743-1794) had originally proposed this law. When he
heated mercuric oxide, the oxygen that was released could not be seen.
But Lavoisier was able to trap it and show that it was made. He proved
that matter was not lost in the reaction. It is very helpful to know that we
neither lose atoms nor make new atoms in a chemical reaction. If we know
what we are starting with (**reactants**), we can look for only those atoms in
what is made (**products**).

We can also predict how much product we will make if we start with a
certain amount of reactant. Companies that manufacture chemicals of any
kind need to be able to do this. They can develop a less expensive process
to make the chemicals, and that keeps the cost down. Then we don't have to
pay more for the things we buy!

The idea that the atoms we have today were the same atoms that
existed thousands of years ago is a strange one. The oxygen atoms
that we are breathing could be the oxygen atoms breathed by George
Washington or Columbus. They could even be the oxygen atoms that
Democritus breathed long ago.

Even more weird is the thought of where the atoms in our bodies
came from. In your body, you could have carbon atoms that were once
in the body of Julius Caesar, the great Roman emperor. Or maybe

you have atoms in you that were once in an eagle that flew over the mountains thousands of years ago. It's strange to think about all of the atoms that we have today being here from the very beginning.

3.5 Energy and mass: two sides of the same coin

Scientists often think of strange things that other people don't worry about. One such scientist was **Albert Einstein** (1879-1955). He was a brilliant scientist who came up with theories that were very hard for other people to understand.

Einstein developed the idea that matter and energy could be converted into each other. It was very difficult to do this, but it was possible. As a result, the Law of Conservation had to be changed to say that matter is neither created nor destroyed, but it can be converted to energy.

We see this happening when stars carry out chemical reactions. Our sun produces heat energy from nuclear reactions that convert matter to energy. This energy allows us to stay warm. Nuclear energy and the atomic bomb are products of Einstein's theory. They use nuclear reactions that produce energy when radioactive particles undergo changes. These very complicated reactions produce light and heat energy.

3.6 Activity

Splitting Atoms
A Philosophy Play
By D.R. Megill

FUNNY BONE ATOM—random atom in the funny bone

BRAIN ATOM—random atom in the brain

Two atoms inside Einstein are discussing their long lives.

FUNNY BONE ATOM: Remember when we lived together in that crazy neighborhood? What was that guy's name?

BRAIN ATOM: Well, we've lived in the same neighborhood, more than once. Which time are you talking about?

FUNNY BONE ATOM: You know, that guy who first noticed us? What was his name? Socialius or Republicus or something like that?

BRAIN ATOM: Democritus, you single-celled ectoplasm. You were part of his high cheekbone, but I was the apple of his eye.

FUNNY BONE ATOM: That's right. Before him, no one even knew we existed. He thought that the atoms in blue things reacted with atoms like you in the eye, to make people see blue.

BRAIN ATOM: That's right. And he thought that some atoms reacted with tongue atoms to produce sweet or sour.

FUNNY BONE ATOM: Do you remember back about 100 years ago when we spent some time in a guy named Dalton? He figured out that we atoms never die and that new atoms are never created. Rather, we are simply rearranged into different forms.

BRAIN ATOM: I wonder if he ever suspected that he shared atoms with Democritus.

FUNNY BONE ATOM: That's a good question. Hey, did you notice that in Democritus, we were pretty liberal. But with Dalton, we became conservative by law.

BRAIN ATOM: You're a laugh riot. But yeah, Dalton called that the Law of Conservation—the fact that we are neither created nor destroyed, but recycled.

FUNNY BONE ATOM: Good thing too. Where would these people be without us? Even this guy, Einstein—He's pretty smart, I gather, but without you and your buddies in his brain, he'd be just another pretty face!

BRAIN ATOM: Let's be honest though. The real question is where would we be without them. We are only atoms, only part of something much greater. Being in people always reminds me that somehow they are more than just the sum of their various atoms. I don't really get how, but while we rearrange and react, they actually grow and change and create and even become, somehow, more than they start with.

FUNNY BONE ATOM: I don't know. We do some pretty cool stuff when we rearrange, making different chemicals and such. Yeah, sometimes we atoms have great chemistry together.

BRAIN ATOM: Seriously, though. What are we but energy and matter? We are always one or the other, but we are never anything that really matters, not by ourselves, anyway. It is only when we are in concert with other atoms that we really amount to anything.

FUNNY BONE ATOM: I was in concert once. I spent some time in Bach's little finger. Boy, did you spend too much time in that Democritus dude. You're way too philosophical.

BRAIN ATOM: Oh, well, looks like we're sloughing off. It's time to split.

FUNNY BONE ATOM: Oh, don't do that! That could be explosive.

BRAIN ATOM: I may be too philosophical, but you've spent too much time in someone who thought she was funny.

FUNNY BONE ATOM: I wonder what they'll figure out about us next. Will they figure out how to turn lead atoms to gold atoms, like they used to try? Or maybe, they'll figure out how to find the sense of humor atom—it's certainly not you!

BRAIN ATOM: Or maybe, they'll figure out how much more they are than the mere movements and collisions of us.

FUNNY BONE ATOM: Give it a rest already! Up and atom, time to go. See you in another mass. Maybe a good Catholic one. I slay me!!!

(end)

3.7 Discussion questions

1. What evidence are you aware of that matter changes?

2. What evidence are you aware of that matter stays the same?

_____

_____

_____

_____

_____

_____

_____

3. Your friends are in an argument about what the trees are made of on your candy planet. One says that they are made of white chocolate. The other says that they are made of dark chocolate. They both are correct. What could you tell them that would encourage them to see each other's point of view?

_____

_____

_____

_____

_____

_____

_____

_____

_____

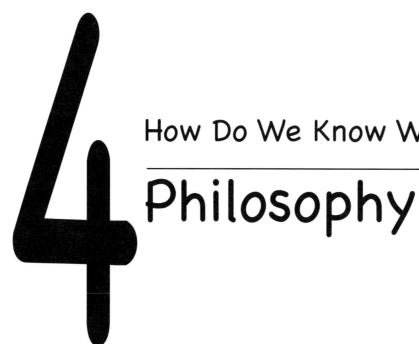

How Do We Know What We Know?

Philosophy

4.1 Introduction

Everybody has questions—that's what helps make life interesting—and for many questions, we can find answers. But when we get answers, we want to know that they are "reliable." That is, we want to know that we are being given the correct information for our questions.

How do we know what the correct information is? How do we know that what we are reading or what we are hearing or what someone is telling us is correct?

There are several ways to check out information. Some of the ways are easy, and some take more work and more time.

One way is to ask someone we trust. If our experience with this person tells us that he or she has been correct in the past, then we can probably trust that this person will give us the correct information.

We could look up the information in a book or in a journal or on the Internet. This works if we can trust the **source** of the information. A source is something that provides information. In science, sources for scientific information are scientists and their experimental data. For journalists, a source can be a person or a written text. For historians, sources can be artifacts, stories, or even personal letters. Sometimes we encounter a published source that is incorrect. When we find something published that is incorrect, we have to check other sources to figure out who is right.

Philosophers spend a lot of time talking about what is true. They also ask the question, How do we know this is true? We have seen how Democritus asked questions about atoms and how Heraclitus and Parmenides asked questions about chemical reactions. Early philosophers called questions about science **natural philosophy.**

4.2 The "Scientific Method"

Scientists ask a lot of questions. They see things around them and wonder about them. How does this work? Why does this happen? What would happen if I did this? These are the kinds of questions scientists ask.

Before the "Scientific Revolution," we did not have good ways to answer science questions. All we could do was discuss the questions. **The Scientific Revolution** (started in the early 1500s) developed the idea of **experiments** to answer scientific questions.

Because of the Scientific Revolution, modern scientists perform experiments to find answers to their questions. They make observations and look for patterns. The explanations they come up with are called "theories." A theory tries to explain what the scientist sees in the lab.

Once the scientist has a theory, he or she develops ways to test the theory. One way is to create experiments that can prove whether the theory is true or false. For example, suppose you have a theory that says that the temperature of water will go up if you put it in the hot sun. If you do an experiment, and the temperature of the water goes down when you put it in the hot sun, that experiment suggests that your theory is not true.

Ibn-al-Haytham
965-1039 A.D.

The Muslim philosopher **Ibn al-Haytham** (965-1039) developed the scientific method many centuries before the Scientific Revolution took place. The scientific method that he developed is similar to the modern scientific method. Both use discrete steps for observing, formulating hypotheses, and testing (using experimentation).

The scientific method was further developed by **Roger Bacon** (*circa* 1220-1292), who added **verification** to the cycle of observation, hypothesis, and experimentation.

Using the scientific method is a way for scientists to evaluate whether the answers to their questions are correct. But sometimes, even when scientists use the scientific method, they cannot be assured that their answers are correct. Furthermore, different scientists will have different ideas about what is correct.

Roger Bacon
circa 1220- 1294

4.3 New ideas in science

Scientists often disagree with each other. There are many theories and ideas that create arguments in science. Most of the time, the arguments are polite, but sometimes they are not.

Everybody holds to certain ideas until there is good reason to change. Sometimes, new information, which presents just a small change to existing ideas, is discovered. Other times, as a result of new information, there is a major change in the way we understand the world around us. That major change is often called a **paradigm shift.** A paradigm is the entire set of beliefs, values, techniques, and ideas that a group of people share. In science, a paradigm is developed over time, and it is based upon scientific information that has been gathered, theories that have been developed, and conclusions that have been reached. Some people change their understanding of scientific information sooner than others. Those who are slow to change resist the new ideas. Sometimes the disagreements can get very heated.

Paradigm shifts have been happening for as long as there have been people. The idea of the paradigm shift was developed in 1962 by **Thomas Kuhn** (1922-1996), a science philosopher and historian. He said that scientific understanding is not a slow and steady stream, but rather, it occurs by shifts in paradigms.

People go along with a prevailing idea until something comes along to really rock the boat. If a new idea represents a major change in the paradigm (how we look at the world), it is usually difficult for people to make the shift.

4.4 Established ideas and paradigm shifts

Before a paradigm shift can occur, new ideas must give rise to new scientific discoveries. New ideas challenge old, established ideas in science. However, in order for new scientific discoveries to happen, new ideas need to be discussed and debated, and the new ideas need to be given the opportunity to challenge the old ideas. When new ideas that challenge old ideas cannot be discussed and debated, new scientific discoveries don't happen.

For example, everyone today knows that the earth rotates around the sun. This is called a **heliocentric cosmos.** (*Helio* is Greek and means "sun." *Centric* is Greek and means "center.") But ancient people believed that the sun rotated around the earth. They believed in a **geocentric cosmos.** (*Geo* is Greek and means "earth.") Going from a geocentric cosmos to a heliocentric cosmos is an example of a paradigm shift.

This shift occurred when **Nicholas Copernicus** (1473-1543) was able to show, by using astronomy, how the earth rotates around the sun. However, the idea for a heliocentric cosmos was proposed almost 2000 years earlier by **Aristarchus of Samos** (*circa* 310-*circa* 230 B.C.)! Aristarchus's ideas were rejected because ancient astronomers and philosophers had strong objections to his ideas. Aristarchus's ideas were not allowed to be discussed because they did not fit with the established ideas for how the world worked. It would be 2000 years before new scientific information could be collected in order to complete this paradigm shift.

4.5 Arrhenius and his graduate committee

New ideas are often rejected, and this can be very difficult for the careers of young scientists who challenge the ideas of established scientific paradigms.

Michael Faraday (1791-1867) discovered ions in 1834. He believed that they were produced only when electric currents were passed through solutions. This was a new and controversial idea.

Svante Arrhenius (1859-1927) used Faraday's idea of ions to explain acids and bases. He wrote about these ideas in his PhD dissertation.

The dissertation was very important. It showed that Arrhenius knew how to do science research. The grade given also told others how important the research was.

The committee that reviewed the thesis did not believe the theory that Arrhenius talked about. Members of the committee felt that Faraday had the wrong idea about ions. They also considered Arrhenius to be incorrect about his research. The committee made Arrhenius change some of his conclusions.

However, he would not change everything that it wanted him to change. Arrhenius believed he was right, and he stood by his convictions. The members of the committee showed that they were unhappy with Arrhenius. They gave him a very low grade on his dissertation. They also said that his work was not very important. The low grade on the dissertation created problems for Arrhenius. He could not get a very good job with that kind of grade. Arrhenius was very disappointed with the treatment that he received from the committee. However, Arrhenius was eventually proven correct. His research was published in 1884, and in 1903, he was awarded the Nobel Prize in Chemistry for his ideas about hydrogen ions.

4.6 Activity

How do you know?
A Philosophy Play
By D.R. Megill

SOCRATES—the great questioner

THOMAS KUHN—questioned the history of science

THOMAS KUHN: Well, I figured out that the best way to study the progress and history of science would be to start at the beginning and walk my way through. So here I am at the beginning, looking for the preeminent of the philosophers: Socrates. There, that must be him now. Socrates is sitting on the ground, reading a papyrus book.

THOMAS KUHN: Excuse me, do you mind if I ask you a question?

SOCRATES: Mind? Why would I mind? Questions are my personal delight, and they are the only path to understanding. I weary of reading anyway, for no matter how many times I ask questions of a book, I get the same answer. What is your question? Perhaps I will prove not quite as stubborn as a book. Or was that your question? Did you simply wish to ascertain how I felt about questions in general? Do you suppose I was too hasty to presume that I wouldn't mind before I knew what the question was?

THOMAS KUHN: Well, I was going to ask if you were Socrates, but I think you must be. Who else could answer a question with four of his own.

SOCRATES: *(smiles)* Who else indeed?

THOMAS KUHN: Actually, the question I have for you is, How do you know what you know? I mean, how do we learn anything?

SOCRATES: Oh, that is indeed a good question. Perhaps we can find out by exploring what we know. What is something you know?

THOMAS KUHN: Well, I know that I'm standing here, talking to you.

SOCRATES: How do you know that?

THOMAS KUHN: Well, I know by the evidence before me. My senses tell me that you are here, for I see you, and my mind tells me that if I see you, then I am here also.

SOCRATES: So you experience it, and you deduce it. Those are, indeed, two prominent ways by which we know things; we know things by our study of the evidence and by our rational minds. Which do you suppose is more reliable?

THOMAS KUHN: Oh, you won't drag me into that argument, Socrates. Many of my day feel that the question of empiricism versus rationalism has been answered by science. We've devised a method by which we systematically study the evidence of our senses and make theories with our minds. We then test the theories by more experimentation and observation.

SOCRATES: Do you mean there are no more questions in your time?

THOMAS KUHN: No. In fact, what I've begun to see is that progress is made by the questions we continue to ask. For each study and theory, a model of the way the world works is developed. I call this model a paradigm.

SOCRATES: Such a paradigm, as you call it, would seem to serve best to point the way to better questions.

THOMAS KUHN: Indeed, for each paradigm, the scientific world as a whole will come to accept it as fact. But some new Socrates always arises to ask better questions—questions that the paradigm does not successfully answer. There is always resistance to such questions, for it is a distressing thing for most people to watch their model fall apart.

SOCRATES: Indeed, I have often felt such changes to be like watching the earth quake or shift under my very feet.

THOMAS KUHN: Hmmm, I like that. Perhaps I'll call it a paradigm quake. That's not quite right. Well, I'll come up with a better term.

SOCRATES: So then, this science is moved forward not by building structure upon structure like a tall building, but rather, by tearing down the structure and starting over?

THOMAS KUHN: Not usually so dramatically or completely as that, but in a sense, yes.

SOCRATES: Then I must ask you what you asked me: How do you know when you have found truth?

THOMAS KUHN: Oh, well, that is the question. Theory, observation, testing, and deducing do seem to work quite well, but only as long as some are willing to continue to challenge the prevailing paradigm and to ask the questions others don't dare.

SOCRATES: So it seems that you must have enough confidence in a given theory to be able to see the questions, but not enough confidence to prevent such questions. It appears to me that what you have arrived at is a way of approximating truth, rather than defining it. And how do such methods find the answers to the most important questions: What is justice? What is piety? What is perfection? What is beauty?

THOMAS KUHN: You're right, Socrates, such questions are not answered well by scientific methods.

SOCRATES: By the way, how do you know?

THOMAS KUHN: What?

SOCRATES: How do you know I am Socrates? You said that you knew by the evidence of your senses and by the reasoning of your mind that you were here talking to Socrates, but how do you know that I am Socrates?

THOMAS KUHN: Oh, well, you told me that.

SOCRATES: Did I?

THOMAS KUHN: Well, I thought you did, but now . . .

SOCRATES: Further, despite your evidence, how could you, Thomas Kuhn, be here talking to me, Socrates? I am long dead by your day. In fact, I have a new theory that I am not Socrates, and you are not Thomas Kuhn. In fact, we are only characters in a script and not really here at all? Or maybe I am wrong, and you have come back to me by way of a time machine, and we really are both here. I wonder how we can know?

Socrates smiles and goes back to reading. Thomas Kuhn shakes his head in a puzzled way as the ground begins to shake under him and the scene fades out.

(end)

4.7 Discussion questions

1. Define paradigm.

_____

_____

_____

_____

_____

_____

2. Think about the paradigm for how air travel works. What major changes would occur if this paradigm shifted? (Could we travel faster, instantaneously, invisibly, etc.?)

_____

_____

_____

_____

_____

_____

_____

_____

_____

_____

3. You are on your candy planet, and you make a startling discovery. You find out that none of the candy contains sucrose (sugar). This will change everything you know about candy. How can you explain to everyone on the planet that candy can exist without sugar?

_____

_____

_____

_____

_____

_____

_____

_____

_____

_____

_____

_____

_____

_____

_____

_____

_____

_____

_____

_____

5

Ways of Seeing the World

Philosophy

5.1 Introduction

We don't all see things in the same way. We each have our favorite sports team or music star or book. People have their own personal preferences, or favorites, that they think are the best.

It's okay to base a lot of decisions on preferences. You may want a hamburger for lunch; that is a preference. A preference, like preferring hamburgers, doesn't have to be justified by anything other than the fact that you like hamburgers.

However, there are many things in the world that depend on more than preferences, likes, dislikes, and beliefs. We may prefer flying to walking, but we don't have the option of saying, I don't believe in gravity. If we walk off a cliff, gravity will show itself whether we believe in it or not. Because gravity is real, we would be experimentally demonstrating the reality of gravity by stepping off a cliff!

5.2 The development of empirical thinking

We have talked a lot about the early Greek philosophers and how they thought about the world around them. The early ideas of the atom were just ideas. There was no way to see whether the ideas were really correct. Many early philosophers believed that something was true as long as their arguments seemed logical and sounded right.

Aristotle (384-322 B.C.) was a Greek philosopher who helped to change the way people thought about the natural world. He believed that we should emphasize what we could perceive with our senses. Aristotle conducted his studies in a very hands-on manner, and he used many different kinds of animals and sea creatures in his studies.

Aristotle
(384-322 B.C.)

The idea of natural philosophy came mainly from Aristotle. Reality in the physical world, according to Aristotle, was what we could experience. Aristotle rejected the approach of Plato and other philosophers who were satisfied with ideas alone. Aristotle wanted to discover what was real through experiences; he did not want to just believe in ideas.

Natural philosophy involved the study of the workings of nature. Observations would be made. Conclusions, that were based upon the observations, would be drawn. Astronomy is an example of a natural philosophy. People could look at the stars and planets and make measurements of orbits and locations, but they could not do "experiments" on the planets. When drawing conclusions, they could use only the information that they had obtained through their observations.

Observations allow people to use the technique of **inductive reasoning**. When employing this type of reasoning, a person draws conclusions from a small number of observations. For example, if some students observe that three different ice cubes are cold, they are using inductive reasoning when they draw the conclusion that all ice cubes are cold. Inductive reasoning has its limitations. We may not look at enough different situations to see all of the possibilities. I can believe that all cats are black if that is the only type of cat I have seen. We know there are other kinds of cats that are not black. So inductive reasoning might sometimes lead to false conclusions.

Inductive reasoning takes observations of one or a few to draw conclusions about many or all.

Three ice cubes are cold; therefore, all ice cubes are cold.

Francis Bacon (1561-1626) was one of the people who used the inductive reasoning method successfully. His studies contributed to the "scientific method." Bacon's approach involved looking at information obtained by observations and then coming to conclusions based upon the observations that were made.

Francis Bacon
1561-1626

5.3 Seeing patterns in the data

Francis Bacon and others made important scientific discoveries. They developed experiments and measured many processes. However, in order to make general conclusions, they needed a tool that they could use to see the patterns that their data created. **René Descartes** (1596-1650) developed such a tool for scientists to use. The tool he developed was the **graph**. Descartes was a scientist, a mathematician, and a well-known philosopher.

Descartes studied many things in his life. He wrote books about optics and meteorology (the study of weather). He also did work in geometry. In addition, his work in mathematics made it possible for others to develop the mathematics field of calculus. An important mathematical contribution made by Descartes was the merging of algebra and geometry. He disagreed with the ancient Greeks regarding the way they did geometry proofs. Descartes wanted a way to measure the lengths of lines in geometric figures. The graph that Descartes developed allowed us to do many things. We could look at both positive and negative numbers. We could also draw figures on the graph and describe them mathematically.

Descartes
1596-1650

5.4 About graphs

Graphs are very useful for studying lab data. By utilizing a graph, we can easily see how quickly (or slowly) something changes when we perform a specific experiment. A graph also allows us to see whether the change is regular and smooth or whether it shifts suddenly. And a graph makes it easy to see the direction of the change; is there an increase or a decrease?

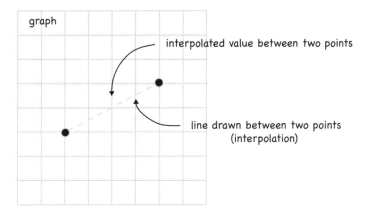

Graphs are a form of international science language. With a graph, anyone can see the trend in an experiment. We don't need to speak the same language to understand how the experiment went.

Graphs also allow us to determine specific data points that are in between the ones we have. We can **interpolate** between two points, and in doing so, we can find out what a value might be without having to go into the lab and measure it.

Graphs can also get us into trouble. If we see a straight line, we might assume that it continues to be straight. But we may not have run enough data points. The line may curve at some point, and we wouldn't know it.

5.5 Modern science and empiricism

This emphasis on observation of the natural world led to the idea of **empiricism**. This philosophy says that all ideas are to be tested against only the natural world. This means that only data from the senses are acceptable. If we cannot see, taste, feel, smell, or hear something, science will not consider it to be real.

Modern science operates on the idea of empiricism. This approach works for some areas of life, but it seriously neglects many important aspects of who we are and why we exist. Some things can't be seen, tasted, smelled, touched, or heard. For a long time, atoms could not be seen or observed. If empiricism had been the only tool of modern science, it is possible that we might not have believed in atoms!

5.6 Activity

Charting a Course
A Philosophy Play
By D.R. Megill

YOU—Faithful reader and student

DESCARTES—Our guide in our quest for clarity

SOCRATES, PLATO, ARISTOTLE, FRANCIS BACON, HUME, BERKELY, AND OTHERS—Various points on the chart

YOU: Oh, boy. There are so many philosophers and so many ideas. If there were just a way to keep them straight. How can you tell who's right and who's not?

DESCARTES: I comprehend, young pupil. I, too, am occasionally disconcerted by the preponderance of theories and disconnected concepts and by their lack of verifiability.

YOU: Was that supposed to help? I have no idea what you just said!

DESCARTES: I agree with you. We need ways to evaluate all of the information we receive.

YOU: Oh, that's better.

DESCARTES: One useful tool is a chart. Look here. I've lined up all of the philosophers and scientists from all of history, and I've placed them in appropriate places on the chart.

YOU: What?! How did you do that?

DESCARTES: Ah yes, well, such are the benefits of being a conceptual character in an imaginative play, but it's best not to dwell on such things for too long. Anyway, this chart ranges, not in order through history, but from rationalist to empiricist.

YOU: You're losing me again.

DESCARTES: *(sighs)* Yes, sorry. Well, throughout history, there have been those who believed that the mind was all that we needed to arrive at truth. Others believed that the senses (taste, touch, smell, sight, and sound) were enough to discover truth. So the left side of this line shows those who rely mostly upon the mind's ability to reason; the right side is for those who rely mostly upon the truth of their senses. We call the left side rationalism, and the right side, empiricism.

YOU: But you need both, don't you? I mean, we have to think about what we see, and how can we think about what we haven't seen?

DESCARTES: You are one very bright student! Yes, of course, you're right. Thus, the chart. You'll see that very few people are on one end or the other, but most are closer to the middle. Plato is pretty far left, but even he recognizes the need for material to reason with. Hume, over there, is about as far to the empirical side as one can get (although a few, like Berkeley, somehow manage to get just a bit further), but even he, reluctantly, recognizes that there are some things that cannot be empirically proven.

YOU: Okay, but how does this chart help us? It's still an awful lot of information!

DESCARTES: Yes, indeed it is. Perhaps it will help if we just walk the line and speak with a few on the chart.

Descartes walks down toward the right side of the line.

DESCARTES: Ah, here's an interesting one: Francis Bacon. He not only falls on the empirical side of the chart, but he helped to clean up the ideas too; he helped by defining the ways in which we could use our senses to test and to observe the way things worked.

YOU: Who's that he's following behind?

DESCARTES: Ah, yes, that's Aristotle. Indeed, in many ways Bacon follows after Aristotle. Aristotle strongly suggested that the truth of even universal ideas could be best discovered by the study of empirical truths. He was very thorough and systematic about his research. Bacon, in building upon Aristotle's groundwork, began to define what we call the scientific method. This scientific method makes it possible for almost anyone to follow the same sort of procedures.

YOU: You mean I can use the scientific method, even though I am not a scientist?

DESCARTES: Indeed, the best philosophers and scientists bring us tools and methods that can be used by practically anyone to find truth. My chart here is one such tool.

YOU: It does help to see them lined up like this. But does the scientific method really work for everything.

DESCARTES: No, actually, it doesn't. Look at these guys far over on the empiricist side. Here's Hume, for example. He pointed out that, in fact, empiricism doesn't really, in and of itself, prove the value of inductive reasoning.

YOU: You're losing me again.

HUME: Let me try. Descartes always was more complicated than he need be. See this pebble I hold?

YOU: Yes, of course.

HUME: What will happen if I let go of it?

YOU: It will fall to the ground.

HUME: How do you know this?

YOU: Because that's what rocks do.

Hume drops the pebble, and it falls.

HUME: Hmm. You were right. It did fall. But how do you know that is what rocks do?

Hume picks up the rock and holds it out again.

YOU: I was right, wasn't I? I know it's what rocks do because I've observed them do so, over and over. Others have observed it too. In fact, I've never heard of anyone who has observed a rock hover in mid air.

HUME: So, you are telling me that you know that every other time a rock has been dropped, it has fallen. But how do you know that it will fall this time? I mean, you haven't experienced that, have you? You have only experienced it fall before. You have not yet experienced it fall this time.

Hume drops the rock. It falls again.

YOU: But I have now. So I was right.

HUME: You were right, but only because your senses tell you that now. It was not your senses that told you that before the rock fell, but inductive reasoning. Inductive reasoning is a product of not only the senses, but also of the mind.

YOU: But... that doesn't make any sense.

DESCARTES: *(leads him along the line to the left)* You asked if the scientific method could prove everything. Hume is simply indicating one weakness of strict empiricism; without inductive reasoning, it tells you nothing about the future. Few people are as strict as he is. Bacon was certainly not as strict an empiricist as Hume. Bacon believed that inductive reasoning was a necessary part of the scientific method. *(Descartes steps into line a little to the left of the middle.)* Socrates, over there, almost at the end of the left side of the chart, would further point out that empiricism and the scientific method will tell you nothing about justice or goodness or piety. He's right, and I would argue (as I take my place in line here) that there are some things that we just know to be true, without any empirical proof at all.

YOU: So where do I fit in this chart?

DESCARTES: Well, that's something for you to decide, isn't it?

YOU: Well, I think I'll go right here. *(walks down the line towards the side of ?????)*

(end)

5.7 Discussion questions

1. Define empiricism.

_____

_____

_____

_____

_____

_____

_____

_____

_____

_____

2. Are there advantages to basing science on empiricism?

_____

_____

_____

_____

_____

_____

_____

_____

_____

_____

3. Are there disadvantages to basing science on empiricism?

_____

_____

_____

_____

_____

_____

_____

_____

_____

_____

_____

_____

_____

_____

_____

_____

_____

_____

_____

_____

_____

4. On the candy planet you have discovered a new kind of sweetener that is not sugar (sucrose). This is why the candy tastes like candy, even though it does not contain sucrose. You discover that this new sweetener is very nutritious and good for your teeth. Using the scientific method and inductive reasoning, how could you convince others of the existence of this new type of sweetener?

_____

_____

_____

_____

_____

_____

_____

_____

_____

_____

_____

_____

_____

_____

_____

_____

6

Seeing the Unseen

Philosophy

6.1 Introduction

We may find it hard to imagine how people in other times understood the world around them. Today we have many tools that we use to explore what we cannot see with our eyes directly. In ancient times, it was not possible to look at things the way we can today.

If we want to know what that thick, dark stuff bubbling up from the ground is called (oil), we can use science tools to find the answer. By using specific techniques, we can separate the oil into different parts (called fractions). We can then study the chemical and physical properties of each fraction. After we learn about each fraction, we might want to separate the fractions in order to use them for different purposes. We can get gasoline, kerosene, and other useful products from the oil. Today we know how to separate a mixture like oil, and we know how to create useful products from the various parts. However, people did not always know how to do things like separate oil into fractions. The idea that matter

was made of mixtures that could be separated was useful for the ancient Greek philosophers.

6.2 Matter as mixtures

The Greek natural philosophers spent a lot of time observing the world around them. They spent a lot of time thinking about the physical material they saw. What was matter, and how did it come about?

Before the Greek philosophers, there were other thinkers from other cultures. The Indian, Asian, and Middle Eastern philosophers also thought about the world around them; they, too, wondered what the world was made of. We usually think of modern science as coming mainly from the Greek philosophers, but it is possible that many of the Greek philosophers were influenced by Indian, Asian, and Middle Eastern ideas.

We have seen already how there were major disagreements between the Greek thinkers regarding what the world was made of. **Parmenides** (*circa* 515-*circa* 450 B.C.) was, perhaps, the first Greek philosopher to think about the physical world we live in. He was born around 515 B.C. into a rich family. Parmenides chose to become a philosopher instead of becoming involved with the family business.

Parmenides
circa 515-*circa* 450 B.C.

One major idea that Parmenides had was that matter could not be created or destroyed. He also believed that all matter was made up of one type of thing, as opposed to being made up of different types of things. This idea did not fit with people's common observations of the world because when people observed their surroundings, it appeared as though everything was made of something different.

Empedocles (*circa* 490–*circa* 430 B.C.), as we saw in chapter one, was a Greek philosopher who created the first periodic table. He was also very involved in politics in his home town of Acragras, a Greek city in Sicily. He felt that Parmenides was wrong about the composition of matter; he thought that matter was a mixture of basic elements. Like Eastern philosophers that pre-dated him, Empedocles believed that there were four elements that made up all matter: *earth*, *air*, *fire*, and *water*. Empedocles called these four basic elements "roots."

6.3 The four elements

Original primitive matter was believed to be affected by the properties of hotness and dryness. The opposite properties of coldness and wetness were also involved in affecting matter. The combinations of hotness (or coldness) and wetness (or dryness) affected original primitive matter, thus giving rise to the formation of the four elements. According to Empedocles, fire and water were opposites of each other. They did not have any properties in common. And, for the same reason, earth and air were opposites of each other.

Empedocles believed that each of the four elements existed in an ideal, pure form, but that these pure forms did not exist on earth. He believed that all of the things on earth were mixed forms of the four pure elements and were, therefore, impure.

The idea that all matter was composed of a mixture of air, water, fire, and earth persisted for 2000 years. Today we know that matter is made of atoms. However, the idea that matter was a mixture of basic elements was useful for understanding the world around us. In some ways, both Parmenides and Empedocles were right! Matter is made of one thing (atoms), and it is also made of a mixture of things (different atoms).

6.4 Activity

Getting Something from Nothing
A Philosophy Play
By D.R. Megill

PARMENIDES—believed that "nothing" cannot be, that there is no change, and that what we see is not what we get

EMPEDOCLES—believed that things change all the time and that we can learn much from what we see

EMPEDOCLES: I have been having this argument with you for the last three hours, and I can get nothing out of you!

PARMENIDES: Your frustration is hardly my fault. First, you claim to be getting nothing from me. However, that cannot be possible, for nothing cannot be a thing at all, and it cannot exist.

EMPEDOCLES (hitting his head with his hand in frustration): What?!

PARMENIDES (ignoring Empedocles): Second, you speak of time as if it is something that is progressive.

EMPEDOCLES: Time indeed seems to stand still with you around, Parmenides!

PARMENIDES: And third, your frustration at the unchanging nature of our conversation is sad, because it is part of the very nature of all things that they are unchanging. If they were to change, they would have to move into the void.

EMPEDOCLES: This conversation is something I'd like to a-void next time!

PARMENIDES: What is not cannot be what is.

EMPEDOCLES: Oh, wait. Now you're starting to sound like my family.

PARMENIDES: (surprised, looking at Empedocles for the first time) I am?

EMPEDOCLES: Yeah, they're all politicians, remember. You're starting to talk like them. Although come to think of it, they are constantly stating that what is not, actually is, so maybe you're not so similar after all. Look, Par, your assertions, besides being patently and obviously false to our senses, are simply unhelpful to any scientific progress. We are the foundation for years of science to come. Technology depends upon our being able to make predictions about the way things work and about how things are put together. Further, technology depends upon the ability to use science as a tool to make more and better tools. Your philosophy will never get us there. We really need to be spending our time figuring out what this world is made of. It seems to me that we should be able to tell from observation, what kinds of interactions are going on beneath the surface (for example, between hot and cold or between soft and hard).

PARMENIDES: Aren't you getting just a little anachronistic there? How can you possibly know what's coming in future years of science.

EMPEDOCLES: It's called poetic irony, and it's perfectly appropriate for characters like us to speak this way in the postmodern era in which the author lives. He's used the device several times for comic effect. You claimed revelation from some mysterious goddess in nature, so don't get to precise about outside revelations at this point! Anyway, speaking of points, we should get back to ours.

PARMENIDES: Indeed, you were accusing me of introducing a philosophy that would stifle technology, but it just so happens that my philosophy will be foundational for Plato, from whom comes all major Western philosophy for many centuries to come! (See, I can do it too—poetic irony indeed!)

EMPEDOCLES: But aren't you acknowledging that there will be progression and change in the future?

PARMENIDES: Only the illusion of such change. Just as there is such an illusion now. Here's the point, Emp: if things changed, it would require that something which currently is, would have to, at some point, become something that is not. If you change, what you were no longer exists. How can you say that there is something which no longer exists. By definition, if it no longer exists, it isn't.

EMPEDOCLES: Hey, I almost got that argument! But here's what you're missing. What if these changes are made because each thing that changes is really made up of other things, and all that really changes is the arrangement of such things. For example, perhaps everything is made of four primary elements: earth, air, fire, and water. If this were true, changes would consist of how these things interact and how pure they are when they interact (how hot, how cold, how soft, and how firm). In this way, the changes would be, somewhat perceptual, as you would say, but would also be real.

PARMENIDES: But you are requiring the elements themselves to change. Nothing can be created; nothing can be destroyed. All is as it is. Nothing changes Empedocles, nothing.

EMPEDOCLES: Certainly not this conversation! Well, somehow, without change, we've none the less covered all the points we needed to make for this chapter! Which means I get to leave!

PARMENIDES: It is interesting that poetic irony allows me to point out that while this conversation has an appearance of flow, of change, it is truly only a static script, stuck in place. Indeed, no matter how many times it is read, this conversation does not change. So you see, it is a perfect example of how the illusion of change and movement does not equal the reality of change and movement. Which means, friend Empedocles (grinning evilly), that you are stuck here, with me, in this conversation forever.

EMPEDOCLES: Nooooooo!

Will Empedocles ever be rescued? Will revision of this text prove the existence of change? Will Empedocles revert to one of the four elements in order to enact change? Stay tuned. . .

(end)

6.5 Discussion questions

1. Empedocles and Parmenides see things from different points of view. Like many philosophers and scientists, they don't agree. In your own words, describe how Empedocles and Parmenides see "matter." Then explain what they are arguing about.

_____

_____

_____

_____

_____

_____

_____

2. Without looking at the next chapter, how do you think Empedocles and Parmenides could resolve their dispute?

_____

_____

_____

_____

_____

_____

_____

3. On the candy planet, an argument breaks out about whether sugar is made of one thing (sugar) or a mixture of things. How could you resolve this disagreement?

_____

_____

_____

_____

_____

_____

_____

7

More About Mixtures

Philosophy

7.1 Introduction

In chapter six, we began talking about matter and its composition. Early humans had some useful categories for matter. However, these early people did not know what these materials were made of. They knew about fur for making clothes, and they knew that certain plants and animals were good to eat, but they did not know the composition of fur or plants.

7.2 Atoms and compounds

We have learned about some of the first ideas proposed by philosophers regarding what makes up matter.

We learned how **Democritus** came up with the idea of atoms. Democritus also believed that atoms could connect with one another to form compounds.

Democritus
circa 460–*circa* 370 B.C.

One important idea that Democritus proposed about atoms had to do with their *primary qualities*. A primary quality was something like size or weight. Democritus thought that atoms had size, shape, and weight. He also said that atoms could move. However, according to Democritus, atoms did not have *secondary qualities*. Secondary qualities, he said, were things like color and taste. Democritus believed that atoms could not have a color or a taste, so an atom could not be green or taste sweet.

Democritus did not believe that compounds were real. He thought that the properties of compounds were due to the properties of the atoms in the compounds. He believed that the way the atoms behaved would determine how a compound would behave.

We also learned that the Greek philosopher **Empedocles** put forth the idea to his fellow Greek philosophers that all matter was made up of four elements: earth, air, fire, and water.

Empedocles
circa 490–*circa* 430 B.C.

The atom theory of Democritus was a good insight into how matter worked. However, **Plato** and his student, **Aristotle,** rejected Democritus's theory of atoms. Instead of developing the idea of atoms, Plato and Aristotle worked on Empedocles's idea that all matter was made up of earth, air, fire, and water. Many people believe that this held science back for centuries.

7.3 The four elements return

As we have already seen, **Plato** was one of the most famous Greek philosophers. He lived in Athens, and he founded a well-known academy called the School of Athens, or the Academy. This was a place where people could learn not only philosophy, but also how to debate.

Plato
circa 427–*circa* 347 B.C.

Plato was interested both in the physical world and in geometry. He combined these two interests in his four element theory. Plato laid out the elements in a geometric form, and he used that form to explain the properties of each element.

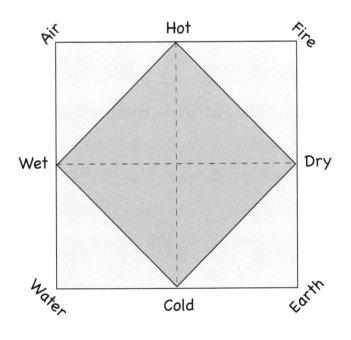

Recall that the original idea of the four elements was not Plato's. In Greece, the idea started with Empedocles, but Empedocles may have gotten the idea from Asian or Indian philosophers. Regardless of the origin of the idea, Plato developed the concept, and Plato's student, **Aristotle**, added to the theory.

Plato believed that there was an original "primitive" matter that had no special or distinctive characteristics. The four elements arose out of the matter as the result of certain properties. In other words, each of the four elements was created because of different, specific properties.

Two of the properties were hotness and dryness. Their opposites were coldness and wetness. The amount of each of these properties in the system determined the properties of the matter that could be seen.

Also, Plato believed that there were no "pure" elements in this world. The pure form of each element could not be found on earth. Matter that we could see here on earth was made up of impure, mixed forms of the four elements.

7.4 The four elements in everyday life

So how did this work? How did the effects of hot (and cold) and dry (and wet) affect the matter on earth? Let's look at a couple of examples. The ancient Greeks believed that smoke was primarily a mixture of air and earth, but that it also included some of the fire form. The earth provided the solid portion, and the air caused the smoke to float around. Fire was obviously needed to heat things up.

The ancient Greeks believed that what we saw as smoke was not real smoke, but an impure, ideal smoke. Real smoke was something that we could not detect. Plato believed that we saw only a mixture of properties that our minds accepted as smoke.

We could also look at a fire that is heating a pot. The pot turns black on the bottom. The pot also gets hot. How did the ancient Greek philosophers explain the heating, blackening pot in terms of the four elements?

The Greeks said that the real fire was a mixture of ideal fire and ideal earth. The fire shared the property of hotness, and the earth shared the property of coldness. When the fire entered the pot, it gave the pot more of the property of hotness. The earth was an impurity in the fire. The earth also had the property of coldness. As the earth gained more coldness, it came out of the fire. The earth was then left behind on the bottom of the pot. This "left-behind" earth was black soot.

Another piece of this idea that all matter was composed of four elements was that the four elements were able to move. Fire moved outward, away from the earth. Earth moved inward. Air and water were somewhere in the middle. The Greeks explained the evaporation of sea water with these ideas. If sea water was heated in a pot, the water absorbed the hotness and the fire. The material then moved away from water and became air. Earth was left behind as salt when the water absorbed enough hotness to move away.

To think about matter in this way can be confusing to the modern mind, but it does show how the Greeks, and other earlier cultures, were able to think about the world around them and to find explanations.

7.5 Plato's shapes of elements

Plato added to the idea that all matter was composed of four elements by talking about the shapes of the elements. He believed that each element had a certain shape and that the shape of each element determined its properties. For example, Plato thought that fire was shaped like a tetrahedron (a pyramid with three sides and a triangular base). The sharp points of the tetrahedron gave it speed. These points also made it feel like arrows hitting the skin.

Plato thought that the earth was shaped like a cube. The cube shape made the earth very solid. Water was shaped smoothly like

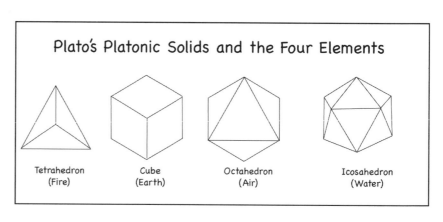

Plato's Platonic Solids and the Four Elements

Tetrahedron (Fire) Cube (Earth) Octahedron (Air) Icosahedron (Water)

an icosahedron (a three-dimensional shape with twenty faces), and air was an octahedron (a three-dimensional shape with eight faces). Plato believed that the shape of each element had some effect upon how that element behaved. Today we know that the basic elements, atoms, do not have platonic shapes, like pyramids or cubes. However, atoms do combine with other atoms, and their shapes do determine how they behave. Proteins are shaped differently than carbohydrates, and salt crystals are shaped differently than diamonds. So although Plato's ideas about water, fire, earth, and air may sound odd to the modern mind, his thoughts about matter having shapes that explained their properties were not completely wrong.

7.6 Activity

The Four Elements
A Philosophy Play
By D.R. Megill

EMPEDOCLES—credited with the four elements theory (and recently escaped from the previous play)
DEMOCRITUS—developed the idea of atoms
PLATO—added geometry to the mix
ARISTOTLE—Plato's student
YOU—the student

PLATO: So you see, young student, everything is affected by deeper (more fundamental) properties. In the physical world, everything is affected by the shapes (mathematically precise and perfect shapes) of the elements. Fire is shaped like a tetrahedron; thus it spreads with speed and destruction. In this way, these four elements cause all the effects we see.

ARISTOTLE: But what is the origin of these four elements. What begins their beginning?

PLATO: You ask the right questions, Aristotle. You are a good student. These elements themselves are not the beginning. As you know, all things come from the nonphysical world of ideas, but even physically, I suspect that these are not the first order. Ari, are you paying attention to me, Ari?

ARISTOTLE: I'm sorry. I thought I saw. . . wait, yes, look. There's someone peeking in over there.

EMPEDOCLES: *(comes forward from the shadows)* I've made it! I've left that blasted conversation with Parmenides. And I knew it—you are talking about my four elements. It's I that influenced you, not Par!

PLATO: Who are you?

EMPEDOCLES: I'm Empedocles. The idea that all matter is made up of four elements is my idea.

PLATO: I was not aware that ideas belonged to any one person. What a preposterous idea. How could there be such a thing as intellectual property rights! Such a thing could never be!

ARISTOTLE: How could you be Empedocles? That's not possible!

EMPEDOCLES: Well, not the real Empedocles, but the real Aristotle didn't speak English either.

PLATO: Think not too long upon that, Aristotle. It is a strange world in which we live. Okay, so you're Empedocles. I am indeed happy to meet with you. I have some questions about your four elements, as you see them, and I have some suggestions as to how to refine them.

EMPEDOCLES: Of course. I am glad to see that Parmenides has been forgotten in the dust of the very change that he denied.

PLATO: Parmenides? Our father, Parmenides? Oh no, not forgotten. He had some peculiar ideas about change and movement, to be sure, but he is deserving of some respect, nonetheless. The truth is that you and he presented two sides of an important debate. He was thesis--things don't change. You were antithesis—things do change. It was someone else who provided synthesis.

DEMOCRITUS: That would be me. My recognition of atoms allowed me to see that the ideas of stability and change could both exist simultaneously. Atoms provide an almost infinite number of stable, tiny pieces that move and interact in various ways in order to effect, at least, physical change.

ARISTOTLE: Why are you here?

PLATO: I suspect that the author wanted four elements in this play in order to mirror the whole idea of the four elements, which is the theme. It has something to do with desiring poetic symmetry to go along with the poetic irony. He's a very eclectic author. I don't care much for poetry myself, but I appreciate symmetry. I don't, however, appreciate the atomic theory much.

DEMOCRITUS: More to your loss. I've not time for such small minded approaches. I'm off.

ARISTOTLE: So much for symmetry.

PLATO: Not so. When one element moves away, it often leaves something behind (as it is absorbed or as it absorbs the other elements). What, perhaps, did Democritus leave behind?

YOU: Well, I often feel left behind when I read Democritus!

PLATO, ARISTOTLE, AND EMPEDOCLES: You!

PLATO: Yes, our faithful student has been left behind. Symmetry remains. Truly though, you have not been left behind. You are here with us in the proper position; you are poised to learn, to explore, and to question. We hope you are enjoying your experiences in science and our minor diversions in these plays.

YOU: Thank you. Sometimes they are a bit odd, with all this poetic irony, but it is fun to actually be part of them now and then!

ARISTOTLE: In the next chapter, we will discuss the question of what life is. This seems a very important question. Clearly your life outside this script is very different from our lives inside this script. Are there differences in the forms of life—plant, animal, human? What are the characteristics of life? Now that we've explored questions of material, it might be good for you to think a bit about the question of life as you move into the next chapter. See you on the other side!

(end)

• 7.7 Discussion questions

1. Using the four elements (air, fire, water, and earth) and their properties (hot, wet, dry, and cold), make a guess as to how Empedocles or Plato may have categorized the following mixtures.

butter

_____

_____

_____

ice water

_____

_____

_____

smoke

_____

_____

_____

rocks

_____

_____

_____

dirt

_____

_____

_____

_____

2. Describe how Plato or Empedocles might have tried to separate one or more of these mixtures. Remember, they did not know about the properties of atoms or molecules.

_____

_____

_____

_____

_____

_____

_____

_____

3. On your candy planet, you need to do an experiment to resolve the dispute about whether or not candy is made of sugar. What experiment could you do to prove or disprove that the candy is made of sugar?

_____

_____

_____

_____

_____

_____

_____

_____

8 What is life?
Philosophy

8.1 Introduction

The changes that carbohydrates undergo, in order to make energy, are not ordinary chemical reactions. They are reactions that take place in living systems. But what is living? What is this thing called "life"?

This is a question that both scientists and philosophers still argue about today. Everyone is aware of life, but it is hard to define what makes something alive and where life came from.

The Greek philosophers thought a lot about life. The philosopher **Aristotle** (384-322 B.C.) believed that only a living being had a soul in it. He called this soul a "moving principle." Aristotle felt that plants, animals, and humans had moving principles. For plants, the functions of the soul were nutrition and reproduction. For animals, the functions of the soul were nutrition and sensation (or feelings). Human souls had these two functions, as well as the function of reasoning. Aristotle saw this idea of the

"moving principle" as the "ladder of creation." He placed plants at the low end because they had less soul in them. Animals were next on the ladder, and humans were at the top.

Hippocrates (*circa* 460-*circa* 377 B.C.) was an early Greek physician. He said that life was caused by the ether. This ether was a type of fire that always existed; it was present in air and in other matter.

Galen (*circa* 129-*circa* 199 A.D.) was a Greek physician who studied anatomy. He further developed the idea of life having a "moving principle." He called it the **vital spirit**. Galen studied anatomy and the organs of the body, and he believed that the vital spirit moved in the bloodstream. The idea of a vital spirit lead to the idea of **vitalism**.

8.2 Vitalism

The idea of vitalism has a long history. Vitalism is the belief that living systems contain a special "something" that non-living systems do not have. Many people believed that the "something" was the soul. Hippocrates and others following him thought that the vital forces associated with life were the **humors**. The humors were black bile, yellow bile, phlegm, and blood. The differing amounts of humors in different people determined their personalities and behaviors.

8.3 Chemistry and vitalism

Many chemists had ideas about vitalism. The French chemist **Nicolas Lémery** (1645-1715) taught that there were three different types of chemical compounds. He said that compounds could be animal, vegetable, or mineral. The category depended on where the original compound was found.

Another French chemist interested in vitalism was **Antoine Lavoisier** (1743-1794). Lavoisier studied the question of compounds, and he felt that the animal and the vegetable types of compounds could be combined.

The Swedish chemist **Jöns Jakob Berzelius** (1779-1848) developed the classifications "organic" and "inorganic." Organic materials were changed by heat into something new. Inorganic chemicals could return to their original state after heating. Only the organic chemicals were considered to contain the vital force.

Louis Pasteur (1822-1895) studied processes related to life. He looked at the fermentation of sugar. Pasteur found that fermentation took place only when living cells were present. He also learned that fermentation could happen only if there was no oxygen present. Pasteur called the process "life without air." This experiment told Pasteur that the process was a "vital action."

8.4 Vitalism begins to crumble

By the beginning of the 1800s, the idea of vitalism was strong. We knew a lot about the chemical compounds in living matter. Although we could isolate and study these chemicals in the laboratory, they were thought to be special; they were thought to possess a vital force. By 1773, one of these chemicals had been isolated from urine. Uric acid was known to be made by living beings. It was not found in dirt or other inorganic sources. It was believed that uric acid was a chemical that had the vital force.

Friedrich Wöhler (1800-1882) was a German chemist and physician who lived during the 1800s. He made urea in the lab by accident in 1828. Wöhler was trying to make an inorganic compound. He wanted to make the compound ammonium cyanate. Wöhler used silver cyanate and ammonium chloride in some of his experiments. The ammonium cyanate that he wanted to make was quickly changed to urea by heat in the experiment.

We now know that the body does not make urea the way Wöhler did. Our bodies make urea using a complicated set of reactions. These reactions were discovered in 1932 by **Hans Krebs** (1900-1981) and his medical student, **Kurt Henseleit** (1907-1973). Wöhler soon realized what he had done. He had made an organic ("living") chemical from two inorganic ("non-living") chemicals. This fact began to change how we looked at the natural world around us. The vitalist idea did not disappear all at once. Many years passed before most scientists took a different view of living systems. There are scientists today who are once again talking about vitalist ideas.

8.5 Reductionism and vitalism

One of the philosophical ideas that has driven modern science is **reductionism**. Reductionism is the belief that you can understand something by taking it apart and understanding each part. For example, if you didn't know what a bicycle was, then you could take it apart, and by understanding the tires, the spokes, and the gears, you could understand a bicycle. But modern science appears to be moving away from reductionism today. Biologists are seeing that the single cell is so much more complex than they had thought. The cell was once believed to be "a bag of enzymes." We now know it to be a very complicated structure with thousands of parts that all work together.

Scientists who work with the brain also see something bigger than the laws of chemistry and physics. They see a mind that can work in ways that we just cannot understand with just chemistry and physics. The brain is a new area for research into life. Because of these observations, we are seeing a rebirth of vitalism and a recognition of how complex life really is.

8.6 Activity

This is your life!
A Philosophy Play
By D.R. Megill

ARISTOTLE—taught that only living beings had souls within them

HIPPOCRATES— early Greek physician who believed that all life was caused by ether

GALEN—Greek physician who believed that the vital spirit was in the bloodstream

BERZELIUS—Swedish chemist who developed the idea of organic and inorganic compounds of chemistry

YOU—student

LÉMERY—proposed the idea that all things are animal, vegetable, or mineral

SOCRATES— Greek philosopher who was always listening for great questions

AUTHOR—the person who wrote this play

ARISTOTLE: Welcome back, YOU! This is your life!

YOU: This isn't my life. This is a play. And I wonder who's in this one? These plays, with all their anachronistic characters and poetic irony, have been getting a bit complicated.

ARISTOTLE: These plays appear complicated and dynamic, but they truly are not. Once set in print, they become stagnant, predictable, and unmoving. But life is complicated. Inside everything truly living, there is movement. In fact, it is the movement, the never stagnant aspect of living things, that makes them living. Every living thing has a moving principle, a reason for being, a purpose. It is not merely a fluke of history that we scientists and philosophers and mathematicians reason throughout our lives. Reasoning is the very essence of our lives. Lower forms of life have narrower movement; they have less reason for being, for moving.

YOU: Whoa, that's scary.

ARISTOTLE: What's scary, my young student?

YOU: I think I actually understood what you said!

ARISTOTLE: *(smiles)* That is because you, my young pupil, are a higher order of life; you are capable of reason. As for who else is here, let's take role. Hippocrates!

HIPPOCRATES: Here. Yes, I am here, although I'm not sure exactly where here is. I do know, though, why I'm here. I'm here because I have some good to do and some harm to avoid doing. I also know how, sort of. I am here because I have been formed from the ether, as all life is.

ARISTOTLE: Galen!

GALEN: Here! Did I hear a discussion of life! Young student, be assured that life is in the blood. The great sages have always said so, and a study of anatomy confirms it. When one loses too much blood, one loses his or her life. It is the blood that moves in the human body, and it is where the vitality of one lies. Even plants have a blood of sort in their sap. Rocks do not have blood.

ARISTOTLE: Lémery!

LÉMERY: Here! Galen is right, mostly. There is a definite difference in the vitality of living things as opposed to nonliving things. It's a chemical thing, though. It's just like the game, twenty questions; things may be classified as animal, vegetable, mineral, or not alive.

ARISTOTLE: Berzelius!

BERZELIUS: Here! The correct terms are organic and inorganic. Organic things are living, and they have the vital life force in them. Inorganic things are nonliving; they include things like rocks and dirt.

ARISTOTLE: Wöhler?

ARISTOTLE: Wöhler?

BERZELIUS: He's not here. He's busy trying to see if he can turn this inorganic play into a living play.

YOU: Are you saying this play isn't alive? I feel alive.

ARISTOTLE: It doesn't seem to be moving too quickly.

BERZELIUS: Seriously though, no. It's about complexity, as we said. The complexity of the real you, the three-dimensional you, is so much more unique, beautiful, and rich than the two-dimensional version of you that is contained in a play like this. Rest assured that the same is true of us as well.

YOU: Oh, I see what you mean. But if life is so complex, then what is it? What makes it life?

ARISTOTLE: The moving principle, the soul, if you must.

HIPPOCRATES: The fire in the ether.

GALEN: The vital spirit in the blood.

HIPPOCRATES: The humors.

YOU: Really? You have to be funny to be alive? Maybe that's why they say that a crowd that doesn't laugh is a "dead" audience.

HIPPOCRATES: I fail to see what you're saying.

YOU: It was a joke.

HIPPOCRATES: Oh? I don't get it.

YOU: Ironic.

HIPPOCRATES: Well, anyway, I meant that the humors are certain substances in our blood, which can make us gloomy or happy, passive or passionate.

BERZELIUS: Are you referring to the chemical nature of things? Whether something is organic or inorganic. That is the nature of life.

ARISTOTLE: As you can see, we all agree, except poor Wöhler perhaps, that life is something that is distinct and that belongs only to living things. Life may be a vitality, a soul, a circulating blood, a purpose, or a principle. It is something distinct and definite, yet complex.

SOCRATES: What is life? That's a great question.

YOU: Where'd you come from?

SOCRATES: I felt drawn by the presence of a great question, one that we could chew on for many a long hour. Let me ask you, young pupil, what is life?

YOU: Well, I'm not entirely sure I could define it right now. It seems that most of you are right; it's distinct and clear, and yet it's complicated and difficult. I also know I have one, which means it's time for me to leave this play before it runs out of steam, before it becomes the stagnant thing it will be when it's done being penned, before--

AUTHOR: Hey, come back, YOU! Rats! It's always bad when you lose a reader before you've even finished. Well, until next chapter, faithful student!

(end)

8.7 Discussion questions

1. Describe how the philosophical idea of vitalism shaped the scientific study of molecules that are found in living things.

_____

_____

_____

_____

_____

_____

_____

_____

_____

_____

9.4 Basic and applied polymer research

Research on polymers is a combination of basic and applied approaches. Some scientists are primarily interested in fundamental polymer chemistry, and others are more interested in what can be done with that chemistry. It's not always easy to separate basic and applied research. Sometimes the two approaches overlap.

Carl Harries (1866-1923) was a German chemist who studied polymers. He worked on long chain polymers, and he discovered that rubber polymers formed rings. **Hermann Staudinger** (1881-1965) was another scientist who studied long chain polymers; he also found that some polymers formed rings. Both of these men were primarily interested in polymers as chemical compounds. They wanted to know what the structures were and how the polymers were made.

Leo Baekeland (1863-1944) was another scientist who studied polymers, but he was more interested in the products that he could develop. He learned some information about polymers (that we could call basic research), but his main purpose was to make a product that he could market. He created the first purely synthetic plastic, and he called it Bakelite.

Both basic and applied research have always been important parts of the scientific process. Scientists working in the same lab may do both kinds of research at the same time. The goal is always a better understanding of the world we live in.

9.5 Activity

Who Cares?
A Philosophy Play
By D.R. Megill

GOETHE—German writer

YOU—student

MARY SHELLEY—author of the novel *Frankenstein*

FRANKENSTEIN—fictional character created by Victor Frankenstein in the novel *Frankenstein*

SOCRATES—philosopher who sought to understand the world by observation and rational thought

ARISTOTLE—made many observations of the world around him

GEORGE MALLORY—wanted to climb Mount Everest "because it is there"

PLATO- student of Socrates

GOETHE: Why do we seek to learn? Why is knowledge so precious to us?

YOU: You're a new one. Who are you?

GOETHE: See, already the search for knowledge begins. Why do you wish to know who I am?
Why does it matter?

YOU: Um, well, I've found that in these weird plays, the characters chosen are not usually arbitrary, but there is a purpose to knowing who the speaker is. Also, it seems that these plays run until certain points are made, and I was thinking that we could get out of here sooner if I could figure out the point sooner. Normally I'd hang around, but LOST is about to start.

GOETHE: Hmmm. So, there is a reason for your search. Well, I am Goethe. I wrote a story about a man who sold his soul to the devil in order to have great knowledge. He did not seek any particular knowledge. He merely sought knowledge for its own sake. Some knowledge seems definitely worth pursuing, because it enriches us and teaches us. History, for example, teaches us a great deal. But what about the quest for knowledge just for its own sake. Are we willing to pay the devil when it's all said and done?

GEORGE MALLORY: Personally, I think knowledge is like a mountain. We climb it because it's there. We climb it because we can. We climb it so that we can get a better vantage point, a better perspective, if you will.

YOU: Some people have died climbing Mount Everest.

GOETHE: Good point! Indeed.

MARY SHELLEY: Boo!

YOU: *(jumps)* Who are you?

MARY SHELLEY: Did I scare you? I like to do that. I'm Mary Shelley. I wrote a book called *Frankenstein*.

YOU: Frankenstein? The monster with the bolts in his neck in the movies?

MARY SHELLEY: *(frowns)* Hardly. In my book, he was made of various parts, but he did not require bolts to be put together. He was articulate, and he was capable of noble feeling. My story of Frankenstein is not a ghost story. Rather, it provokes philosophical thinking and discussion about the nature of life, about science, and about whether we should pursue all scientific ends just because we can.

GOETHE: Indeed. The question of life, which you've been studying, is a good example. Is it best that we know everything about it? The more you know about life, the more thorny the questions become. Questions of cloning, stem cell research, and so on. Just because we can do these things, should we?

YOU: Maybe the problem is that we don't know enough, not that we know too much. Perhaps, in the past, we quickly dismissed questions about souls and life because there was no practical technology to come from them. Perhaps we were afraid of the technology which could come.

FRANKENSTEIN: Boo!

YOU: Yeah, like him. But, maybe if we'd pursued a better understanding of life and the soul, we'd now be better equipped to understand these types of questions and to make better decisions about such technology. Maybe all science shouldn't be applied science. Perhaps it is worth pursuing basic research now, in order to prepare for applications which may come later.

GOETHE: Or maybe some knowledge is just too difficult for us. And maybe certain fields of science, like some mountains *(casts a glance at Mallory),* should not be climbed.

YOU: I can go with that. Can I go watch TV now? That's an applied technology I approve of!

ARISTOTLE: Hold on, slow down. Let's examine this a little more carefully.

YOU: *(groans)* Oh, it's never quick when you arrive. The only person that takes more time than you is . . .

SOCRATES: Boo!

YOU: Yeah, him.

ARISTOTLE: So the question is why we pursue knowledge. We observe the world around us in order to better understand its purposes, its mechanics, and its applications.

SOCRATES: And yet, we ought to also be observing the world in order to understand how concepts of purity, justice, and so on can be applied as well. We observe what we see in order to understand what we don't see. Isn't it worthwhile to pursue such knowledge, even though the application is not immediately clear?

YOU: Wait a second. You two are just continuing the argument that started way back in the very first play!

PLATO: I did tell you then that their arguments were endless. Still it's interesting, isn't it? We've come full circle. We have as many questions about our questions as we do about the answers. Why do we want to know? Is it always best to know? How do we know what we know?

MARY SHELLEY: But what does this tell us about the proper use of science? Should we pursue knowledge for it's own sake? Should we create a monster if we can, because we can? Should we create life if we can, because life is precious? Should we destroy life if its destruction can lead to better applications and understanding? What if it's only plant life or animal life?

GOETHE: Does the end ever justify the means?

SOCRATES: These are all extremely good questions. Let's explore them. It shouldn't take more than a few centuries.

YOU: Or better yet, I am going to do an experiment. I'm going to see how many pieces of applied technology I can use at once. I'm going to turn on my TV, listen to my iPod, read a book, relax on my couch, talk on the phone, and . . .

GEORGE MALLORY: See! Those are all examples of the good that such pursuits of knowledge have brought. And don't forget other pursuits that have truly improved human life: machines and medical advancements, among others.

GOETHE: I am not arguing that knowledge is bad or that scientific pursuit is unwarranted. I am simply exploring the limitations and the dangers of a constant pursuit of knowledge, whether it is for its own sake or whether it is in the interest of applied advancements.

YOU: Well, I've just invented a joke (or maybe I'm just applying it). Knock, knock.

MARY SHELLEY: Who's there?

YOU: Boo!

MARY SHELLEY: *(jumps)* Boo who?

YOU: You don't have to cry, but I am leaving now.

You exit, and thus the play ends.

(end)

9.6 Discussion questions

1. Do you think basic research is important for applied research? Why or why not?

_____

_____

_____

_____

_____

_____

_____

_____

_____

2. Do you think applied research is important for basic research? Why or why not?

_____

_____

_____

_____

_____

_____

_____

_____

_____

_____

_____

3. Philosophers and scientists sometimes have trouble respecting each other's viewpoints. Describe how being open to an opposing viewpoint is helpful for science.

_____

_____

_____

_____

_____

_____

10

Chance, Purpose, and Life
Philosophy

● 10.1 Introduction

Many people believe in something greater than themselves. All societies have had a sense of the supernatural. This supernatural being was (or is) believed to have some kind of control over the daily lives of individuals.

Many people also believe that there is some kind of purpose in life. Things happen for a reason. These people don't like the idea that there are just random occurrences with no purpose behind them.

Scientists sometimes have a hard time with purpose. We use the idea a lot, but we are not always sure what we mean. We can say, The sodium atom prefers to give up an electron to form the sodium ion, but what does that really mean?

10.2 Greek philosophy - cause & effect

The early Greeks developed a religion with many gods and goddesses. These beings were believed to be the cause of many things that people could see. It was believed that some of these beings controlled different parts of nature.

There was a god of the wind. Another god was responsible for the lightening people saw. Different beings had charge of the natural world, and people had no way of understanding them.

Then many Greek philosophers begin trying to explain what they saw in nature by reasoning with their minds, instead of simply believing in gods. **Anaxagoras** (*circa* 500-*circa* 428 B.C.) believed that clouds being split by the wind produced lightning. He did not think that lightning was produced by the god Zeus.

Anaxagoras
circa 500-*circa* 428 B.C.

Anaxagoras felt that the mind influenced all living things. He taught that the mind was infinite and unchanging. This mind entered into and controlled all material objects. Anaxagoras also taught that all matter was made up of atoms. So Anaxagoras and other philosophers of his time replaced the action of the supernatural beings with the action of the mind. They did not see any need to include the gods in their science.

10.3 Aristotle's four causes

Aristotle developed the idea of "four causes." Many people say that these causes form the basis of science today. He believed that every change was caused by something else.

Aristotle
384–322 B.C.

Imagine a bowl. Aristotle could show four causes for a bowl. The first cause for a bowl was the **material cause**; the bowl was made of clay (for example). The second cause was the pattern, or model, for the bowl. This was called the **formal cause**. Aristotle would have said that the formal cause of a bowl was "bowl-shaped."

The third cause was the **efficient cause**. The efficient cause dealt with how the bowl came into being. The potter made the bowl out of clay. So the potter (the maker) was the efficient cause.

The last cause is called the **final cause**; it was the purpose of a thing. The purpose of the bowl might have been to hold breakfast cereal. Aristotle felt that this was the most important cause of the four.

Our word "teleology" comes from the Greek word for "cause." The word is used to explore the ideas of design and purpose in nature. Something occurs a certain way because there is a purpose in that process or structure.

10.4 The idea of purpose

It didn't take long for others to disagree with Aristotle. **Epicurus** (341-270 B.C.), another Greek philosopher, was one such challenger. Epicurus taught that the goal of life was to achieve the absence of pain and fear. He believed that all events were the result of atoms moving in empty space.

Epicurus
341-270 B.C.

Lucretius
circa 99-*circa* 55 B.C.

Lucretius (*circa* 99-*circa* 55 B.C.) wrote a poem called *De Rerum Naturae (Concerning the Nature of Things)* to argue for this philosophy. Lucretius promoted the Epicurean philosophy in his poem. He argued that the gods did not have any control over the world around us. Lucretius taught (as did Epicurus) that everything we saw could be explained by the random and purposeless motions of atoms and collections of atoms.

Cicero
circa 106–*circa* 43 B.C.

Cicero (*circa* 106–*circa* 43 B.C.) was a Roman politician and philosopher. He wrote *De Natura Deorum (On the Nature of the Gods)*. In this book, he argues for the existence of design and purpose in the world. Cicero said,

When you see a sundial or a water-clock, you see that it tells the time by design and not by chance. How then can you imagine that the universe as a whole is devoid of purpose and intelligence, when it embraces everything, including these artifacts themselves and their artificers?

In summary, some philosophers believed that the world around them had design and purpose to it. Others believed that the world had no design or purpose to it; they felt that the movements of atoms and collections of atoms were adequate to explain life.

10.5 What about today?

Over two thousand years later, we see the same discussion happening today. One big difference between then and now is that we know more about the world around us. Science has shown us some of the complexities of the universe and of life.

There are many people today that agree with Anaxagoras, Epicurus, and Lucretius. They believe that we are the result of random actions of atoms and molecules.

Others see the world the way Aristotle and Cicero did. These people see how complex a protein is and how many different functions proteins have. They see the information in DNA that carries the pattern for cells and organisms. They believe that this information suggests strongly a design for life and a purpose.

The debate will continue as long as there are people to debate. As we have seen throughout this workbook, philosophical ideas influence scientific study. The controversy over new ideas and the arguments around these new ideas is a necessary part of science. These arguments are good for science because they provide fertile ground for new discoveries.

10.6 Activity

What's the Point? The Curtain Call
A Philosophy Play
By D.R. Megill

List of characters

LUCRETIUS	ARISTOTLE	EMPEDOCLES
SHAKESPEARE	AUTHOR	PARMENIDES
DESCARTES	FUNNY BONE ATOM	BRAIN ATOM
ANAXAGORAS	CICERO	LEUCIPPUS
YOU	XENOPHANES	MALLORY
DEMOCRITUS	SOCRATES	
EPICURUS	SARTE	
PLATO	ROSENBLATT	

We see a stage. The stage is full of a crowd of people. All of the actors that we've seen in the previous plays stand here, ready to take their bow, for this, the final play. If you look closely, you can see that Aristotle and Socrates are still arguing. There's Empedocles, who is trying to get away from Parmenides. Oh look, there's Einstein's funny bone atom, arguing with his brain atom. In addition, there are Leucippus, Mallory, and of course, YOU. There are even a few new faces; is that Shakespeare? Let's listen in on the whispered discussions as they wait to take their bow.

LUCRETIUS: Why are we here? Where are we now? Why do we stand? And why do we bow?

SHAKESPEARE: All the world's a stage, and all the men and women merely players.

DESCARTES: I believe the series of plays that we are in has run its course, and we are now "bowing out," as it were.

ANAXAGORAS: That's nonsense. You speak as if we are merely puppets in some grand scheme . . . as if the gods have written our lives for their whimsy.

SHAKESPEARE: They have their exits and their entrances; and one man in his time plays many parts.

ANAXAGORAS: Who invited him?

DEMOCRITUS: It matters not. Anaxagoras, for once, is right. Our interactions have simply been random, albeit strange, encounters. There is no purpose to them at all.

YOU: But I thought the purpose was to help me learn.

EPICURUS: It is always the nature of man to believe that the world revolves around him, but it is not so. However, it is our blessed lot to make the most of the world. We must enjoy what is there to be enjoyed, and we must avoid that which is undesirable. That's why I haven't been here before--I've been avoiding it.

YOU: But no, that makes no sense. How can these plays be the result of random interactions. They've been odd, but they've all had a purpose. They've all made a point. They can't be just the result of random encounters.

SARTE: Oui, it is indeed tempting to believe in purpose, but it is merely an illusion.

PLATO: But what about all the poetic irony? That would seem to point to an author outside our own existence in this two-dimensional plane.

ROSENBLATT: Irony is dead.

ARISTOTLE: I think we killed it! We've certainly beaten it enough!

AUTHOR: I've practically gone hoarse over it, I must admit.

FUNNY BONE ATOM: Ah, so we're beating a dead Hoarse, are we? And still they do not stop, as irony sharpens irony, eh?

YOU: So, the theory is that these characters all simply float around meaninglessly until they bump into each other, that the dialogues are simply comprised of the letters that randomly float around until making some illusion of sense, and that the AUTHOR who occasionally speaks is lying or is a figment or something?

CICERO: That hardly seems likely. Think of the complexity involved in bringing the right characters into the right conversations at the right times. And to further increase the complexity, these characters just happened to make salient points at precisely the right places in this book. All this seems very unlikely to have happened without intent. I think the gods must have planned these encounters.

XENOPHANES: It is more likely that we are imposing the points upon our own conversations. We are creating, through our discussions, ideas that we believe to be important, and then we are attributing them to some mysterious author.

SOCRATES: How, friend Xenophanes, do you know this to be true? How do you know the reverse is not the case?

PLATO: Indeed, I suspect it is more likely that we are only approximating the true ideas in our discussions. Our two-dimensional discussions are merely shadows of the truths that are out there. So there is a pattern for our discussions, and they are not completely random.

DESCARTES: Mostly I think I'm inclined to agree. The fact that we are all sharing this experience indicates that it is, by some definitions, real and that reality extends beyond our own creations. It seems there must be someone above and behind these shared ideas.

ARISTOTLE: All of this started somewhere, indeed. There must be some prime mover behind it all.

YOU: Hmm. This is quite a lot to think about. I can see that so many of our questions come to this: Do things happen by design or by random interactions? If you'll all excuse me, I have some thinking to do.

SOCRATES: Thinking? Not running off to check out the TV?

YOU: No, just to think. Whether it was your created purpose or the random result of your interactions, you have done this for me; you have caused me to think, and I thank you. (bowing)

All the characters bow.

LUCRETIUS: Were these plays pointless, or were they pointed? Are we random thinkers, or were we anointed? And now we all wait with breath that is baited; were these poems accidental or strictly created?

AUTHOR: I know that I'm here, and I bid purposeful adieu. Whether the plays hit their mark, I leave up to YOU. I suppose as I bow out, when it's all said and done, I hope to your learning they added some fun. A little whimsy never hurt any task, and answers come only to those who will ask. (*Slowly, the lights fade. The stage and its members recede into the darkness. Only YOU are left standing in the light.*)

AUTHOR: For while it may not be true in life, in these plays, it has all ultimately been about YOU.

YOU: The end.

(end)

10.7 Discussion questions

1. Why do you think the debate over purpose has been going on for centuries?

_____

_____

_____

_____

_____

_____

_____

_____

_____

2. Is it useful for science to look for purpose? Describe why or why not.

_____

_____

_____

_____

_____

_____

3. What do you think? Is there purpose to the universe? Why or why not?

_____

_____

_____

_____

_____

_____

_____

_____

Pronunciation Guide

Abdera	(ab-ˈdē-rə)	
Acragas	(ˈä-krä-gäs)	
Aegean	(i-ˈjē-ən)	
Anaxagoras	(a-nak-ˈsa-gə-rəs)	*circa* 500–*circa* 428 B.C.
Anaximander	(ə-ˈnak-sə-man-dər)	*circa* 611–*circa* 547 B.C.
Anaximenes	(a-nak-ˈsim-ə-nēz)	*circa* 585–*circa* 525 B.C.
Archimedes	(är-kə-ˈmē-dēz)	*circa* 287–*circa* 212 B.C.
Aristarchus	(a-rə-ˈstär-kəs)	*circa* 310–*circa* 230 B.C.
Aristotelian	(a-rə-stə-ˈtēl-yən)	
Aristotle	(ˈa-rə-ˈstä-təl)	384–322 B.C.
Arrhenius, Svante	(ə-ˈrē-nē-əs, also ə-ˈrā-nē-əs, ˈsvän-te)	
		1859–1927
Baekeland, Leo	(ˈbāk-land, ˈlē-ō)	1863–1944
Bakelite	(ˈbā-kə-līt)	
Bacon, Francis	(ˈbā-kən, ˈfran(t)-səs)	1561–1626
Bacon, Roger	(ˈbā-kən, ˈrä-jər)	*circa* 1220–1292
Berzelius, Jöns Jakob	(bər-ˈzē-lē-əs, also bər-ˈzā-lē-əs, yäns ˈyä-käp)	
		1779–1848
Cicero	(ˈsi-sə-rō)	106–43 B.C.
Copernicus, Nicholas	(kō-ˈpər-ni-kəs, ˈni-kə-ləs)	1473–1543

Dalton, John		1766-1844
Democritus	(di-ˈmä-krə-təs)	*circa* 460-*circa* 370 B.C.
Descartes, René	(rə-ˈnā, dā-ˈkärt)	1596-1650
Einstein, Albert	(ˈīn-stīn, ˈal-bərt)	1879-1955
Elea	(ˈē-lē-ə)	
Empedocles	(em-ˈpe-də-klēz)	*circa* 490–*circa* 430 B.C.
Ephesus	(ˈe-fə-səs)	
Epicurus	(e-pi-ˈkyūr-əs)	341–270 B.C.
Euclid	(ˈyū -kləd)	*circa* 325-*circa* 265 B.C.
Faraday, Michael	(ˈfa-rə-dā,ˈmī-kəl)	1791-1867
Galen	(ˈgā-lən)	*circa* 129–*circa* 199
Goethe	(ˈgər-tə)	1749-1832
Harries, Carl		1866 - 1923
Henseleit, Kurt		1907-1973
Heraclitus	(her-ə-ˈklī-təs)	*circa* 540–*circa* 475 B.C.
Sir Edmund Hillary		1919-2008
Hippocrates	(hi-ˈpä-krə-tēz)	*circa* 460–*circa* 377 B.C.
Hume, David	(hyūm)	1711-1776
Ibn al-Haytham	(ˈib-un al-ˈhī-tham)	965-1039
Ionian	(ī-ˈō-nē-ən)	

Kekulé von Stradonitz, Friedrich August

(ˈkā-kū-lā fun ˈshträ-dō-nits, ˈfrē-drikh ˈou-gūst)

Krebs, Hans	(ˈkrebz, hanz)	1900–1981
Kuhn, Thomas	(ˈkūn, ˈtä-məs)	1922–1996
Lavoisier, Antoine	(ləv-ˈwä-zē-ā, än-ˈtwän)	1743–1794
Lémery, Nicholas		1645–1715
Leucippus	(lū-ˈki-pəs)	*circa* 480–*circa* 420 B.C.
Lucretius	(lū-ˈkrē-shē-əs)	*circa* 99–*circa* 55 B.C.
Miletus	(mī-ˈlē-təs)	
Parmenides	(pär-ˈme-nə-dēz)	*circa* 515–*circa* 450 B.C.
Pasteur, Louis	(pas-ˈtər, ˈlū-ē)	1822–1895
Plato	(ˈplā-tō)	*circa* 427–*circa* 347 B.C.
Pythagoras	(pə-ˈtha-gə-rəs)	*circa* 580–*circa* 500 B.C.
Samos	(ˈsā-mäs)	
Socrates	(ˈsä-krə-tēz)	*circa* 470–399 B.C.
Stagira	(stə-ˈjī-rə)	
Staudinger, Hermann	(ˈshtou-ding-ər, ˈhär-män)	1881–1965
Thales	(ˈthā-lēz)	*circa* 625–*circa* 545 B.C.
Whewell, William		1794–1866
Wöhler, Friedrich	(ˈwər-lər, ˈfrē-drikh)	1800–1882
Xenophanes	(zi-ˈnä-fə-nēz)	*circa* 560–*circa* 478 B.C.